W9-BLO-461

MOUNT VERNON CITY LIBRARY

HOUSE MAGIC

Discarded by MVCL

HoUSE
MaGiC

The Good Witch's Guide to
Bringing Grace to Your Space

ARiANA

MOUNT VERNON CITY LIBRARY
315 Snoqualmie
Mount Vernon, WA 98273-4295
(360) 336-6209

CONARI PRESS
Berkeley, California

©

Copyright
2001 by Ariana.
All Rights Reserved.
No part of this book may be
used or reproduced in any manner
whatsoever without written permission,
except in the case of brief quotations in critical
articles or reviews. For information, contact Conari
Press, 2550 Ninth Street, Suite 101, Berkeley, CA
94710-2551. ○ Conari Press books are distributed by
Publishers Group West. Cover Photography © Richard
Waite; house interior by Louise Cotier. ○ Book
Design: Claudia Smelser ○ Author Photo: Stephanie
Beeley ○ Interior Illustrations © Sandie Turchyn

Library of Congress Cataloging-in-Publication Data
Ariana.
House magic : the good witch's guide to bringing
grace to your space / Ariana.
Includes bibliographical references and index.
ISBN 1-57324-568-2
1.Interior decoration—Psychological aspects.
2. Occultism.
NK2113 .A78 2001 113—dc21   2001000761
Printed in the United States of America on recycled paper.
01 02 03 PHOENIX 10 9 8 7 6 5 4 3 2 1

It starts with knowing. . . .
Know your will and will what you know.

BUTCH MILLER

1

CREATING YOUR OWN REALITY

My goal in writing this book is to collect in one place a few of the ideas that I have run across in my practice as a tarot counselor. There is such a diversity of information available from different sources and traditions that I thought an eclectic collection of ideas would help readers take control of their lives by getting their houses in order.

The quotation that serves as the book's epigraph is key to the whole concept of House Magic. Indeed, it is key to any system through which you hope to achieve transformation and the ability to maintain control over your circumstances.

Before you start on any endeavor, you have to know what you want. It can be a general desire, such as wishing for love, good health, or money. Or it can be specific, such as wanting a new house with so many bedrooms on a particular street. Whatever it is that you want doesn't really matter. The key is knowing that you want something.

When I give tarot readings, some people sit right down and have specific questions they are burning to know the answers to. These people often end up with the answers to their questions and more, because they are focused. They are open to interpretation and strategies; their focus on the idea enables them to see possibilities branching off and leading to new ones.

Then there are people who, when they sit down with me, get confused when I ask them what they want to know. "You mean I have to have a question?" they will ask. Nine times out of ten, after talking to them for a little while, I learn that there is indeed something on their minds, and then we can proceed. I will ask them why they came to see me in the first place. Something must have triggered or prompted them to sit down at my table. Of course, occasionally someone will come to me on a lark or will be dragged in by a friend, but usually there is a reason of some sort, on some level—there is a mystery to be solved.

There are a few people, though, who claim they don't want or need to know anything in particular, that they are content with what they have. I often wonder if they aren't just fooling themselves, or perhaps are looking for something more but don't know how to say it or focus on it or understand it. They will still get a tarot reading; after all, they obviously want to know something or they wouldn't be there. But if they were more in touch with their inner desires, if they weren't so afraid to speak their minds, then they would be able to bypass stumbling blocks and live more active, involved, and meaningful lives. Not from the tarot reading alone, but just by how they are as people.

This is part of getting focused and understanding yourself.

It is hard work to look inside ourselves and see the empty hollow places. No matter how happy we are in our lives, our careers, our marriages and families, there are always little holes somewhere that are aching to be filled.

Finding those holes is something only you can do. Becoming self-aware and focused is key to having the will to manifest your desires. How can you bring something into your life if you don't know what you want?

Wanting things, if they are things that will make your life more comfortable, is not greed. Not everyone wants to be a millionaire. Some people find money a nuisance, but they don't want to live in a cardboard box on the street either. We live in a society where we have to have money and material goods, so why shouldn't we do our best to activate the positive energies that will bring abundance into our lives?

You have to believe in what you want. Believe you can have it. Examine the idea of what you want. We are all born naked and alone. We will all die alone. Why shouldn't we make the most of what we can do for ourselves and for others in between? There is no law that says that some people can have everything and other people can have nothing. The truth is, we all deserve to have whatever it is we believe we need.

Almost as important as knowing what you want is knowing how to go about getting it. You have to take action to achieve results. You can't sit around wishing something would happen. You have to go out into the world and get involved. If you want to become a famous writer, for example, you can take writing courses, get a few things published for free on the Internet, write and write every day until it is second nature. By educating yourself about markets and becoming informed about trends, you create your own luck, your own magic, and by doing that, you will ultimately find yourself in the right place at the right time.

That, in a nutshell, is the philosophy of House Magic. You are taking control of your life and your environment. How you choose to do that is up to you. Witchcraft, wishcraft, ancient systems of environmental balance, astrology, moon phases, candles, gemstones . . . all will heighten the possibilities of achieving goals and discovering what you truly want.

Practicing the concepts of House Magic will lead to a lifestyle change. You have already taken the first step in opening your life to an infinite number of possibilities. Just by picking up this book, you show that you desire to learn more about creating a life filled with positive possibilities. *House Magic* provides an overview of systems that have been in use for hundreds, even thousands of years. These systems would have died out long ago if there weren't some truth in what they do.

Is it possible to activate magic in our home, to create the reality we always dreamed about? If our home is our castle, then why not? Why shouldn't our home be the power center for all that we desire in our life and be pleasing to the eye as well?

Gone are the days when witches lived in tiny little shacks in the outskirts of towns, brewing strange potions with jars of bizarre things in their dark little kitchens. We live in modern times. Times when we can embrace the lessons handed down to us from the wise women and men in our past and combine them with the conveniences of modern life. The modern day "witch" can truly have it all: a beautiful home that she decorates as traditionally or as eccentrically as she wishes (using some of the tips that I will lay out), or a place in his community without being deemed "that weird guy at the end of the street."

The sight of a broom on the door does not have to mean a home filled with pentagrams, strange-smelling herbs, and rocks everywhere in sight. There are easy-to-do arrangements and organizational techniques that don't have to invade on the appearance of "normalcy" that you may wish to convey. After all, you want your children's friends to come over and play without their parents wondering what the heck goes on over at *that* house, anyway. . . .

And this is where House Magic comes in. *House Magic* demonstrates, from an eclectic viewpoint, how to activate positive energy flow into your home, and therefore, into your life. You will learn which areas of the home are most important for fulfilling your own personal needs and how to obtain maximum benefit from the energy you create. The theories described are derived from my studies in the esoteric and metaphysical sciences and from my work as a professional tarot consultant.

We all have the ability to control certain aspects of our lives, which manipulates our present and activates auspicious energy for our future. The suggestions presented in *House Magic* are derived from a combination of theories, including witchcraft, Feng Shui, crystal and gemstone work, astrology, first nations, and other theories that explore the balance of Nature and the environment.

The idea behind *House Magic* is to help you create a beautiful and loving home that the whole family can enjoy and to which you can invite company without having to explain yourself!

I would never pretend that my advice is going to help anyone win the lottery or become a millionaire unless that is already in their destiny. But little steps to enhance our daily lives are certainly worth taking. A crystal hanging in the window is not only beautiful; it brings positive vibrations into the room and repels negative ones. You can use crystals to lend auspicious energy to "dead" corners of your home, to absorb negative vibrations from unwelcome guests, to clear the air after a disagreement with a spouse or kids. . . . The uses for crystals are endless as conductors of our energy; the possibilities for application in our own lives can be limitless.

Symbolic ornaments can grace your home. You might select a goldfish or a turtle or a crystal ball. Whatever accents you choose should be placed with care to activate the most auspicious energy you can create.

We can be whoever we want to be. We can no longer sit on the fence watching the rest of the world go by while we remain passive in this adventure that is our own life. Even if you do something as simple as slipping a rose quartz into your bra or pocket, that act projects positive thought into the universe, and as a result you will see the ripplings of positive action coming into play.

Who doesn't love the smell of apple cider brewing in the fall or turkey roasting in the oven on Thanksgiving? And I'm sure we've all had the experience of walking into a house where there is something rancid in the garbage or a cat box that is long overdue for a change. Smells are part of House

Magic too. Smells can inspire us, invigorate us, help us feel more amorous, or relax us. Incense, oils, and scented candles will fill your home with the right scents for your goals.

An altar, your own private sacred space where you can perform affirmations and rituals, will be part of your House Magic plan. Your altar can be as small as a paperback book or as large as a banquet table; it is up to you.

Rituals, spells, and affirmations have been a part of the human experience for thousands of years. Through the action of speaking your thoughts to the universe, you create a flow of positive energy that will enable you to control various aspects of your life. *House Magic* will teach you how to create your own affirmations as well as providing you with examples you can use.

Every human being is unique. We all want different things from life. Some people want to attract love, some want prosperity, some want better health, others want harmony in the home. Whatever it is you desire to enhance your life, you will find a way to activate a positive energy flow and make that dream a reality. House Magic will help you turn your home into a vibrant castle of creativity and warmth, a place to entertain with pride and to nestle away with your loved ones.

With your home life under control, you will be ready to face any challenges the world has in store for you! Gracing your physical space is half the battle; the other half is getting your mind under control. You have to throw out those old tapes of insecurity and self-doubt and make new ones of strength and self-confidence. Not only do you have to believe in yourself and that you can do whatever you set your mind to do, you have to remember that there are rules to follow, just like in any thing you do. For your inner transformation to take place, you have to have respect for yourself and for others, intent for the good of all, and ethics.

Respect

When you undertake any sort of esoteric or spiritual work, a key word to remember is *respect*.

RESPECT YOURSELF

Respecting yourself is the most important thing you can do in your life. Most of us put ourselves last on the priority list of our lives. We put children and spouses and work ahead of our own needs all the time. Women especially are guilty of this. It is time to rearrange your list. Put your own name at the top and then work your way down the list systematically.

You should be number 1. If you don't take care of yourself, how can you take care of anyone else? You have to eat properly, sleep properly, and act with honesty and integrity.

RESPECT OTHERS

Always treat other people with respect. Really *listen* when someone is talking to you. Try not to judge. Try to treat people how you want to be treated. If someone is presenting you with a challenge, send him light and love. Don't spend time trying to figure out how to put a curse on her or zap him with a voodoo doll. That just takes energy away from you and the work you are trying to achieve. Don't take advantage of people. Don't have sex for sex's sake. Try to keep your intimate encounters full of love and light. Be kind to strangers. Smile at people. Spend time with your children and loved ones. Do volunteer work. All in all, try to bring a bit of light to all the people you encounter, even if you don't know them.

RESPECT THE EARTH

We are blessed with Mother Earth. She works in cycles, nurturing and creating, providing us with the elements of earth, wind, fire, and air that we need to survive. She provides us with food and shelter. Respect the Earth by giving back to her. Create beauty by growing a garden, or if you live in an apartment, have plants. Don't litter or pollute. Be aware of the cycles of the day, of the months, of the seasons. Respect all the creatures that share this Earth with us.

RESPECT THE UNIVERSE

We are all connected, somehow, depending on our spiritual beliefs. Every action brings a reaction. Every deed, good or bad, goes toward our karma. Our life on Earth is just one small part of everything else that happens in the universe. Some energy sources are bigger than we are. They go by many different labels: God, Goddess, Spirit, Spirit Mother-father, Angels, Spirit Guides, and so on. You don't need to follow any particular belief system to conduct House Magic. Just believe that there is energy hurtling through the universe, and it is ours to tap into as we need to. Respect the idea of the Creator, of God, for you are asking for help to control your life. Remember to pray and give thanks on a regular basis. Personally, I don't think we need to go to a church on any particular day to give our thanks. God is everywhere, and we should praise him or her whenever we can. If you belong to an organized religion, that is fine. Respect your religion. If you grow disenchanted with it, examine the reasons for this. Give yourself permission to explore another path. Spirituality is a personal experience, and we all learn and grow from it in different ways.

Intent

The idea of intent is very simple: Whatever you want, you can have. You just have to focus and believe in it. Whatever your intent is, it must be for the good of all. Intent in this case is not only your attitude but also your goal. Spells and affirmations work on intent. You will learn how to speak your dreams to the universe while still maintaining free will.

Everything starts with intent. Think about what you really want, what will make your life run more smoothly. Is it more money, a balanced love life, harmony in the home? If you are like most of us, you want a combination of things.

Make a list of all the possibilities you want to explore. Don't worry about having too many; just write them all down. Once you have your list, organize it into order of priority. When you are finished decide which items on your list are the most challenging for you. Which are only a matter of getting your act together and being more organized? Which things have you been putting off but are within your grasp if you would just take the time to deal with them?

Focus on one idea at a time. Sometimes it helps to do

something that won't be too stressful, or to take on something that you have been putting off so that you can have a sense of "Now, that wasn't so bad, was it?" Maybe it's time to revamp your résumé, because with all the new positive energy surging into your life, you just might need it.

Responsibility and Free Will

With intent comes responsibility. I very strongly encourage, and will do so repeatedly, to be careful what you wish for, what you want, what you *think* you want, especially if you intend to cast spells or chant affirmations. You have to be sure. You have to be clear.

You cannot manipulate another person's free will. Allowing others' free will is letting people do what they are going to do without trying to manipulate them with spells. This book will not teach you how to get a certain someone you have your eye on or to obtain property and possessions that belong to another.

Each human being has free will, and none of us has the authority to affect another's free will, even if we think it is for the best. Just because you think that John would be happier with you than with Jane, you cannot cast a spell on John to come to you. This is taking away John's free will, and you don't want to be responsible for the consequences of such an action. However, I will show you how to attract a lover more suited for you into your life.

You know you want love. But you can't force someone to love you. All you can do is ask the universe to send you light and love. If that person is meant to be with you, he will find his way to you. If it is meant to be, it will be.

Never manipulate someone else's free will. I cannot stress this enough and will repeat this point many times.

Neither is it a good idea to manipulate or control another person's energy without their knowledge. This can be very tempting if you have a loved one who is ill. Of course you want to send them healing energy and help them in any way you can. Or maybe you know someone who is having money problems or is in a bad marriage. It is not up to you to decide how they need to conduct their lives. You can ask their permission to conduct a ritual or bless a stone or light a candle for them. If they give their permission, feel free to help in any way you can.

Ethics

Ethics encompasses respect and intent. Be aware of your ethics. If you are creative, you can find ways to manipulate situations without manipulating other people's free will. For example, let's say that your boss is giving you a hard time at work. You absolutely dread going into the office each morning. Instead of trying to think of ways to get rid of the boss or modify her behavior, be creative and direct the thought process at yourself. Try to maintain high moral standards. Ask your Higher Self to help you conduct yourself in such a way that the boss cannot find fault with you. Ask for the ability to do your job in the best possible way, with light and love for all. Don't think about the boss; just think about yourself and how you approach your job. Maybe something in you *has* been rubbing the boss the wrong way. Maybe your boss is going through personal problems of her own that she is projecting onto you. Maybe you really do need to improve your performance. Whatever the reasons you are having this conflict, don't spend a lot of time overanalyzing the why's and wherefore's. Just *be*. Be who you are, and be all that you have the possibility to become.

Try to be aware of morals—your own and other people's. If the Ten Commandments help, then by all means follow them. Don't covet other people's possessions. If you really want something, you can bring it into your life without taking it away from other people.

The Threefold Rule
One important idea to remember is that whatever we send

out into the universe will come back to us three times. This is the threefold rule. We don't know what will come back to us or how. There is no way to know. This is why we have to be very clear on our intent, certain that we want it, and know that its coming to us will not cause harm to others. So whenever you are doing energy work, remember the threefold rule.

We have all seen horror movies or heard jokes in which someone is granted a wish, and then what seemed like an innocuous wish becomes twisted into a nightmare that the wisher hadn't foreseen. You must be careful of that happening.

In my own practice, I stay away from spells that manipulate people or events. Who am I to foresee what is really good for me or what the outcome truly should be? Maybe if things were left to unfold the way they should, the outcome would be desirable. Or maybe that thing isn't meant to be, for me, at this time.

It can be very tempting and very easy to want to cast a love spell on a particular person. I cannot stress enough, please don't. Please do not think that just because you have fallen in love or lust with someone that you can just cast a spell and the person will be yours forever. Many of these situations have backfired.

In one of them the woman wanted the man so badly she did a variety of spells to get him. She got him all right. And then, after a few months, she realized that she did not want him. He was not the person she thought he was. But could she break up with him? No. It was a mess. They fought, and their lives were a nightmare. Eventually they were able to disengage from each other, but by then, the damage was done.

In another case, a woman was conducting voodoo rituals to get the man she loved. They have been together a few years, but not as together as she desired. He is drawn to her, they go out, they travel together, but he still maintains that he wants to keep his own place, that he is not interested in another marriage. The woman, in essence, has the man as she wanted, but she doesn't have him fully and completely. Not in the way she desires. If she hadn't cast spells to entice him to her, would she have eventually found someone else who would love her the way she needs to be loved, instead of this reluctant love in which he cares for her but won't commit?

Stories like this keep me cautious about spell casting because of the unknown quality of the threefold rule. And they should make you cautious too. Who needs to pour energy into a situation that isn't meant to be, forcing square pegs into round holes? That energy could be better used to send out positive vibrations that will echo through the universe and attract the proper person.

Many times throughout this book I refer to different kinds of energy: energy within your environment (yin and yang) and energy within your body (the chakras).

Yin energy is feminine energy. *Yang* energy is masculine energy. The idea is to have a perfect balance of both energies in your home to create harmony.

The *chakras* are points on your body that are energy centers. There are seven major chakras, and a host of smaller ones, located along your spine, which are made up of constantly spinning electrical energy. People have different opinions on several of the chakras, such as where they are in your body and what colors are related to them. Some sources start the chakras at the base of the spine (this makes the most sense to me), and some start at the reproductive organs. In between the base and heart is a whole other arrangement of opinions. The information presented here about the chakras is the information that I use. As with all the ideas presented in *House Magic,* find the information that connects to you, that feels "right" to you.

The chakras can be considered gateways; it is up to you whether or how you choose to open and shut the gates. When we "open" a chakra, we let the energy from that chakra point take over. For instance, if we "open our third eye," we become more in tune with our unconscious energy and may have psychic visions or be able to conduct divination.

When we "cleanse" our chakras with rituals, crystals, meditation, or any other method, this promotes both emotional and physical self-healing. We dispel negative energy that is building up inside of us and disturbing our delicate energy balance.

Chakra Points and Related Colors

The colors that are associated with the different chakras help to activate their energy. One way to activate a throat chakra—such as if you have trouble speaking your mind to someone, or public speaking in general—is to wear something blue, such as a blue choker or scarf around your neck.

TAILBONE (BASE OF SPINE) Red

SACRAL OR SEXUAL CHAKRA Orange

SOLAR PLEXUS Yellow

HEART Green

THROAT Light blue

THIRD EYE (FOREHEAD) Indigo

CROWN OF THE HEAD (SOFT SPOT ON A BABY!) White

Securing Protection

In doing any esoteric work, you need protection from negative energy. Some people may try to steal your energy, especially when you are opening yourself up to altered states of consciousness. Before any meditation or spell, you should protect yourself.

MEDITATION FOR PROTECTION

1 Get comfortable. Close your eyes. Regulate your breathing.

2 Imagine a white light shining down from the heavens, into the top of your head or your crown chakra.

3 Imagine white light flowing through your body, flowing through your veins. You are white light.

4 Imagine the white light flowing through you and into the ground. Some people like to imagine tree roots flowing from their feet into the ground. This anchors you to the Earth.

5 See a blue bubble floating in the air. Watch as the bubble comes closer and closer to you. When the bubble lands near you, go inside of it. This is your bubble of protection. No one can harm you on the astral plane when you are in your blue bubble.

6 Once you are in your blue bubble, continue with the work you wish to do.

7 When you are finished with your work, climb out of your blue bubble. Thank it and send it on its way until the next time you need it.

Another way to protect yourself, if you aren't meditating, is simply to imagine yourself inside a blue bubble. Some people visualize white light surrounding them. Imagining yourself inside a safe zone, such as a bubble or a cloak of white light, is great if you are doing things like tarot readings, visiting sick friends, or dealing with cranky in-laws!

Other ways to protect yourself from unwanted influences include carrying certain stones or doing spells of protection. Obsidian and apache tears are great stones for absorbing negative energy or repelling "psychic vampires"—people who sap your energy or strength. You know the type: that really needy relative or clingy friend. They are the huge egoist who needs constant flattery. They are that overbearing Hollywood movie producer trying to force you to cut a deal you don't want to take. Just the thought of having lunch alone with them drains you. Often people have no idea they are psychic vampires. But some people do know, and these people are even worse. They really will try to drain your energy and use it for themselves, much like "real" vampires drain your blood.

I've done something for protection that seems to be working so far. I bought a blue crystal ball that is flat on the bottom. At the time I bought the ball, I was not thinking at all about protection. All I thought was, "What a cool crystal ball!" since it had some very interesting inclusions—the cracks and bubbles in stones and crystals—in it. Then a situation occurred in my life where I was in need of protection from people who might discover some secret information that I had in my possession.

In a moment of inspiration, I wrote my secret on a piece of paper and placed it under the blue crystal ball. You see, part of the problem with keeping the secret was my own. I'm a chatterbox Aquarian; I knew that I could inadvertently spill the beans in some way, and I didn't want to do that. So, the secret is written, right under the crystal ball where I can see it from my desk. Just the act of seeing the ball and knowing that the paper is under it helps me keep my mouth shut. Using the crystal ball, I am activating the possibility of minimal to no repercussions should the secret be revealed. And of course, like all secrets, it will bubble up to the surface one day. And I hope by then it won't matter any more!

Getting Focused

The most important thing to consider when beginning any form of magic or energy manipulation is getting focused. How can you concentrate on achieving your goals if you have 4 billion thoughts rattling around in your brain? You have to learn discipline, to train your mind to do what you need to do.

The way to do this is through meditation. You have to learn to clear your mind and channel your energy toward your goal. (In chapter 2, "Clearing the Clutter," there is a meditation for clearing your mind.) Once you have a good grasp on getting your mind clear, you will be ready to proceed.

Next, you must focus on honing your intent. The following meditation is good for focusing intent. It forces you to focus and manipulate your mind (for example, seeing the color red).

MEDITATION FOR FOCUSING INTENT

1 Find a comfortable place to meditate. I often lie on the floor by my altar, but sometimes I lie on the couch or in my bed. Some people prefer to sit up, and that is fine too. The key is comfort. Remove confining clothes and distracting jewelry. Sometimes I like to have a stone or two near me or on my third eye or in my hand.

2 Close your eyes. Clear your mind. Focus on your breathing. Slowly count to ten, breathing in and out.

3 When you are fully relaxed, imagine a color. Some people like to use tools like balloons or balls. Whatever works for you. One of the keys to House Magic is doing what works for you.

4 Imagine one color at a time. Is red really red? How red is red? Is it bright red or dull red? Really examine that color. Be that color.

5 Some colors will be easier to see than others. The first time you meditate you might just use one color. Keep building on the colors every time you meditate until there are several you can see.

6 Learn to switch colors. Switch them faster every time you meditate. Maybe you can see two colors at once now. If you are seeing yellow when you want to see red, really focus on seeing that red. Don't let the yellow distract you. You are building will and discipline.

7 When you are done, open your eyes. Very slowly and carefully get up, in case you are lightheaded. Drink spring water to ground you. If you continue to be lightheaded or unfocused, wear a hematite ring to ground you after your meditation.

Finding Your Levels of Consciousness

The deeper you can go into your subconscious or unconscious, the better you will be at manipulating energy and using your will to create your own reality. Some people work with seven levels of consciousness, to indicate the chakras; they go as low as they can, finding new levels all the time, much like unpeeling the layers of an onion. With the mysteries of the human mind, use whatever imagery helps you access these different levels—whether it's elevators, filing cabinets, or chakra points—and visit however many levels you can clearly focus on. In the beginning, it's hard to focus at all, so don't get frustrated if you only go to one or two levels. Mind power takes a lot of discipline. It is better to focus on one or two levels with total concentration than to be floating around several levels, listening to the dog bark and being aware of other distractions in the physical world.

MEDITATION FOR FINDING YOUR LEVELS

One way to build up concentration and psychic energy, to find the level of the unconscious you need to find, is to learn how to find the different levels of thought in your mind. Some people see states of consciousness as filing cabinets or elevators.

1 Get comfortable. Close your eyes. Clear your mind. Don't forget to protect yourself.

2 Imagine white light shining down from the heavens, entering through your crown and filling your body.

3 Once you see the white light, imagine you are getting on an elevator.

4 Your elevator has many floors. The idea is to go down one floor at a time, get off of the elevator and see what is there.

5 At first you might just want to ride the elevator, especially if you are having trouble staying focused. Just be in your elevator and look at the floor numbers. Go down one floor at a time. Don't get off until you get to the bottom.

6 When you get off the elevator, look around at what is there. Really feel and see all that is there, whether it is a beautiful garden or a hellish basement.

7 When you have finished exploring the floor, get back on the elevator and return to where you started.

8 Release your bubble of protection.

9 Slowly open your eyes. Get up and write down images and emotions in a notebook.

Activating Energy

I learned one of my favorite ways of activating energy in a Kundalini yoga class years ago. When I teach theater classes, I often have the students do this as a warm-up exercise. It is also a good icebreaker for parties or gatherings. If you are doing this before performing a ritual or reading for someone, make certain you wash your hands. As a practitioner of metaphysics, you should be washing your hands all the time anyway, to cleanse yourself of negative energy.

EXERCISE FOR ACTIVATING ENERGY

1 Rub your hands together. Rub them lightly, palm to palm, fingers straight, so that they are brushing each other in a rapid manner.

2 Think about all your energy surging into your hands.

3 Feel your hands getting warm and tingly.

4 Stop rubbing your hands and hold them together. Gently and slowly, pull them apart.

5 Feel the energy pull between them.

6 Only pull them as far apart as you can feel the energy.

7 Once you feel the energy dissipate, push them slowly back together until you find where the energy is again.

8 Concentrate on pulling the energy out further.

9 With practice, over time, you will be able to pull the energy as far apart as your arms.

This is a good exercise to show people how the body really is made up of energy and electricity.

↪ DREAM MAGIC

Dreams can be very useful as problem solvers. You can fall asleep, asking for help with a problem, and sometimes the answer will come to you in a dream. Of course, if you dream like I do, many of the dreams are problems unto themselves, as my unconscious struggles to make sense of the world. Some dreams, though, carry very real and meaningful messages. They can help us to break down the blocks that are keeping us from progressing. They can help us understand our problems and learn how to solve them in different ways.

Dreams are also a way that people on other planes communicate with us. It is not at all unusual for dearly departed ones to speak to us in our dreams. Often they are here around us, but we do not see or hear them, so they come to us in our dreams.

Dreams are a reflection of ourselves. If you have a lot of nightmares, you are probably wrestling with many issues or maybe one big problem. You might want to try sleeping with citrine under your pillow. If you claim to not dream at all, then ask to be shown a dream before you go to sleep. You can make dream pillows for more vivid dreams or restful dreams, or for problem-solving dreams. If you have trouble sleeping, chances are that once you use a few tips from the Feng Shui chapter and get your home more balanced, you'll sleep much better!

It can be difficult to understand what dreams mean, and there are many theories on how to interpret dreams. In my practice, when people tell me their dreams I try to understand the dream in a few simple ways.

1 How does the person tell me the dream? The language and emotion the person uses in relaying the dream speaks volumes to me. Why they might tell one part

first, or why does one symbol stick out more to them than another?

2 Was it a story or a clump of images, or were parts of it hazy?

3 What symbols are in the dream? What could be considered symbols in the dream? For example: Is a house in a dream really a house? Is it the home? Is it representing our job or a problem we have? Is it the labyrinth of our unconscious? Is it a journey we have to take? What is the house like? Is it dark and scary or light and homey? Is it the beginning or the end of some quest? Are the doors opened or locked? Are there mirrors? Do the stairs lead anywhere? Do the floors break when you walk on them? Really looking at some of the symbols in your dreams can suddenly give you a *Eureka!* moment. Or maybe it means nothing at all to you. Sometimes a house is just a house, but usually it is something more.

4 What does the dream mean? Sometimes the story of the dream itself is totally obvious. For instance, I once dreamed that I was in an ocean and the waves were swelling higher and higher and I felt like I was on the

edge of some relentless journey and I wasn't afraid but I wasn't too happy either. I suddenly woke up and realized that my water had broken and I was in labor with my first child. But most dreams are not that obvious.

If you are interested in learning more about how your conscious and unconscious connect or don't connect, keep a pen and paper or dream journal or a notebook by your bed. You can record any information, however trivial it might seem, during that twilight period between dreaming and waking. When you wake up from a dream, write it down. Even just writing key words or emotions can give you clues. The more you can discover about yourself, the more you can activate positive energy flow in your conscious life.

✤ NOTE TO READERS

I use the term *Spirit Motherfather* throughout the book, since this is how I speak to the universe. I practice eclectic witchcraft, which means that I draw from many systems for my beliefs and rituals. Wherever I say, "Spirit Motherfather," please feel free to substitute whatever term you desire in accordance to your religion and beliefs. House Magic is nondenominational and can be used by anyone of any belief system. Some words include *God, Goddess, Spirit Guide, Higher Self, Angel,* and any number of names of gods and goddesses.

Creating Your Own Reality

HOUSE MAGIC

House Magic is a way of life. Use it to clean up your home and your mind. Organize your space. Learn how to create positive and harmonious energy flow through your home and body.

MIND MAGIC

Respect yourself, others, the Earth, the universe. and the Spirit Motherfather.

Know what you want, and keep your intent honest. Don't let your immediate intentions or goals blind you to what is good for the bigger picture of balance and harmony.

Activating your personal power doesn't give you permission to intrude on other people's lives. Don't manipulate others.

Try to keep as honest and true to yourself and society as possible.

Whatever you send out into the universe will come back to you three times . . . good or bad!

ENERGY MAGIC

Whenever meditating or doing metaphysical work, create a sphere of protection around yourself.

Learn how to focus your will. Start by doing one thing at a time. Do exercises or meditations that will help you concentrate better.

Activate your energy simply by rubbing your hands together.

DREAM MAGIC

Sometimes your dreams hold the hidden key to your subconscious. Don't overlook your dreams as a source of wisdom.

2

CLEARING
THE
CLUTTER

Believe it or not, before you can begin to utilize House Magic, you have to get organized and clear out the clutter!

Yes, I mean the clutter on your bookcases, the clutter in that laundry pile in the corner of your bedroom, the clutter in your front hallway, and of course, the clutter in your mind. You also need to clear the air, literally, of negative vibrations. As well as clearing your environment, you must pay attention to your body as well. It is time to release physical and emotional baggage that is holding you back from being free to live your life in a full and productive way.

The whole concept of House Magic is to allow energy to flow through your house and not get bogged down. Too many piles of books and papers and toys scattered all over the place block energy. You must get your physical environment under control if you ever expect to harness energy. And if you are involved in mediumship, it's even more important to have clear shelves and regular dusting habits, at least in the room where you work. In mediumship, you need to be able to sense vibrations flowing in from other people and other dimensions. If your home is full of knick-knacks and piles of papers, you might well be drawing on lingering vibrations from other people and events instead of the ones you are trying to focus on. It is even suggested that you bathe before performing any acts of divination, scrying, or mediumship to cleanse your body of energy you may have picked up during the day.

Now, some of you may already be neat and tidy and don't have this challenge, so you can just read the section in this chapter about clearing out air clutter and can skip to the others. For the rest of you, here are some tips on getting started.

❧ AIR CLUTTER

Before you begin your clutter attack, walk around the room you are working in holding a burning sage stick. Walk around the outer edges of the room, holding the stick over a nonflammable bowl of sand, so that when pieces of it fall off, you won't set the house on fire.

As you walk around the room, call upon the Spirit Motherfather to guide you in bringing light and love into your home and heart. Ask for help deciding what to keep and what to pitch. Ask for the negative vibrations to be cleansed from your home. Create your own little ritual. Every time you reach a corner, hold the stick up so that the purifying smoke reaches the topmost ceiling corners. You don't want any negative vibrations stuck in there. You might also want to burn a white candle while you cleanse the air and cleanse the clutter.

If you feel stuck while working on the physical clutter, burn your sage stick and repeat your ritual again. Every time you start a new room, use your sage stick. When you are finished with each room, ask the Spirit Motherfather again to bring light and love into your home and heart, and do your walk around with the sage stick. Thank the Spirit Motherfather. Your room is ready for the next steps in House Magic.

᧨ ENVIRONMENTAL CLUTTER

My name is Ariana and I am a pack rat! Pack rats come in many guises. You are a collector. You are a hobbyist. You are a coupon clipper with piles of coupons you forgot you had because they aren't organized. Perhaps you subscribe to ten or twelve magazines and newspapers. You are a romantic, saving every letter and cocktail napkin from every person you ever dated. You have boxes of toys and clothes that the kids have outgrown because you just can't bear to part with them, or you are saving them for *their* kids. Or maybe you save stuff for a rainy day because you just don't know when you might need it. You have fat clothes and thin clothes and clothes that surely will come back into fashion again, for fashion goes in waves, doesn't it?

You have crates of records because one day you will figure out how to get that stereo working again and, boy, weren't record covers just the coolest? Then there are those jars of pennies and the loose change flung into dressers and jewelry boxes.

Take a good hard look at those things you collect. Really. Why are you collecting them? What do they really mean to you? Do you get enjoyment out of them? Is your collection displayed beautifully or packed away neatly or is it just helter-skelter, thrown all over the place? Are you hoarding items because you can't bear to part with them, or because you're not sure what to do with them? Do you have stuffed animals on your bed because you did as a kid, and you're in the habit of having them there?

You really, really have to look at what you have, what you do with what you have, and who you are. Not who you were. *Who you are right now.* You've seen it on the talk shows: If you haven't worn it or used it in the last three years, get rid of it.

Overwhelming? Definitely. But I'll say it again: To gain control of the energy of the universe, you must gain control of your own environment. You have to know what you have and why you have it. You have to figure out what things you're doing on automatic pilot, what was ingrained in you by other people's habits (like your mom's), and what you really feel about the things you are collecting.

As we go through each subject—papers, toys, knick-knacks—write it down and see what it means to you. A very big part of witchcraft is listening to yourself. How can you ask for possibilities to come into your life if you don't know who you are and what you want or need?

Paper and Collectibles

Here is how I tackled my collections, my subscriptions, my mementos. One tiny step at a time. For goodness' sake, don't say, "This is the weekend I'm going to do this whole house." I'll tell you right now, you won't. Not if you've been a bona fide pack rat your entire time on this planet. Tiny goals. Tiny steps. One thing at a time. Not even one room at a time. One *article* at a time.

Reevaluate your lifestyle and habits before you tackle the backlog. How did you get into this way of being? It's learned behavior; we all do it.

First of all, if you have access to the Internet, do you really need to subscribe to a newspaper? This cleared out a major pile for me right off the bat. I would save papers thinking I could use an article, or the coupons, or I hadn't gotten around to reading it yet but I *will* one day . . . and next thing you know, there's a week or two of papers shoved under the couch. Get rid of them. Read your paper online. Print out an interesting article if you truly think you will ever look at it again, immediately put it in a labeled file folder, and *file it,* either in a filing cabinet or an inexpensive file box.

How about those magazines? How many do you really read? Did you subscribe to most of them thinking you were going to win $10 million? Again, get rid of the paper problem. Use the Internet. When you are finished with your magazine, give it to a neighbor or drop it at your doctor's office or your kids' dance class lounge.

Look around at all the knick-knacks you have. Do you have too many? Do you even dust them? They can be great fun and good conversation pieces, but look at them. Is that chipped dolphin you got from Sea World when you were ten really worth hanging on to? If the answer is a sentimental Yes, pack it carefully and put it in the basement. If the answer is No, donate it to a church sale or Goodwill or just pitch it.

Really look at what is being displayed in your space, for all of it reflects you. How about those book cases? Are there more piles of papers than books hanging out of them? Is there a layer of dust so thick that even the cat sneezes when it jumps on top? I wouldn't for a moment suggest organizing your books alphabetically or by size, but if you get into it, go nuts! Try to keep your bookcases for books, and perch a few of your treasured knick-knacks and crystals and statues in front of them.

Deal with mail as soon as possible. Immediately throw away junk, put bills in a bill folder, letters in your letter folder, and display cards on your mantel.

Handle school papers the same as mail. Read that newsletter, write important dates on a big wall calendar in your kitchen or over your desk, then *throw the newsletter away*. Look at your child's work of art or test. Hang it up, or decide if it is a wonderful indication of brilliance, in which case, put it in a labeled box that stays in the basement, or *throw it away*. Each of my children has a big plastic container I keep their art and school work in. You have to be discriminating, though, especially in the younger grades, or you will have boxes and boxes of yellowing paint blobs. Just choose a few. I'm pretty sentimental about my kids and used to save every single doodle and scribble they ever did. But *why?* Humans are a strange breed. We have to let go. We have to live in the present. Clinging to the past serves us no useful purpose.

Toys

Are you wading knee deep in toys? Those plastic baskets at

the dollar store are great for whipping toys into. Kids these days have way too many toys. Do your kids really play with all of their things? Maybe it's time to fill a box and trundle it · down to the battered women's shelter. The toys won't do anyone any good in a box in the basement waiting for your eight-year-old to have children.

My mom saved a ton of our toys from when we were kids. Sure, it was cool to see them as an adult with kids of my own, but come on. . . . Do you really think a Nintendo-playing six-year-old is going to groove on playing with a mothball-scented puzzle from some TV show he's never heard of? It was a nice thought, but that puzzle would have been better off with a kid from that generation who could appreciate it. Who knows what technological wizardry will be going on when our kids are grown, so let it go. . . . Give it to someone who can appreciate the toy right now. Don't wait for some mythological grandchild who won't appreciate it.

Sure, save a favorite doll or two. We should all save one or two mementos. But not boxes and boxes of them.

I still have trouble with the toy thing. The kids don't; it's me. So here is what I do. Every few months I go through one of the kid's rooms or the playroom with three boxes. In one box—the "good-bye box"—I put stuff that I know they will never play with again and that doesn't have some sort of emotional attachment. The second box is my "sentimental box." I can't possibly get rid of that toy because so-and-so bought it and, oh, it's so cute, and I remember how much he used to laugh when I made it work. Be very strict with yourself about your sentimental box. Think about whether you'll ever even look at it again once it's down in the basement. Or is it like your own little time capsule that you'll look at on your son's wedding day? Whatever it is, consider why you are keeping it. The third box I call "the waffle box." This is stuff I know I should get rid of, but can't bear to just yet, or I'm not sure if one of the kids will suddenly decide they have to have this, and boy, am I a mean mom to give away their *favorite* toy. So I'll put it in this box and take it downstairs. If nothing calls to me in a month or two, or if the kids don't notice it gone, then it's off to Goodwill.

Clothes

Look at the clothes you are accumulating from your children and yourself. Pick out a couple of cute baby outfits for your sentimental box, and then give the rest of the outgrown clothes to charity. Even torn clothes can be used by charities, which sell them to recycling places by the pound (at least they do here in Ontario, Canada).

If you are like me, you probably have a closet full of sliding sizes. "Fat" clothes, "thin" clothes, winter, summer, out-dated-but-maybe-they'll-come-back-into-style clothes, and so on. I spent several years losing about fifty pounds, yet I hung on to some of my "fat" clothes. I'm not sure why. Maybe I was afraid that one day I would wake up and suddenly be fifty pounds overweight again and have nothing to wear! At any rate, it was hard for me, but I managed to get rid of most of those outfits. They are doing me no good hanging there when someone else could be using them.

I have a double-edged sword when it comes to keeping clothes, as one of my jobs is being a theater teacher, and you just don't know when something might come in handy for a costume. I try to keep all costume-type clothes hanging in a separate closet, where I can still see them to remind me what I actually have instead of stored in a box where I'll forget about them. Clothes, hats, and shoes are great for kids of all ages to play dress up in, so donate your excess to amateur theater companies, day care centers, summer camps, and so on.

Some people have a pile of clothes that they will "get around to" sewing or patching. If you haven't gotten to it yet, are you really going to? Fix them or get rid of them.

The same goes for shoes. How many pairs of shoes do you *really* need? I know, I know. Some of you have a shoe fetish, and if that's the case, keep them organized somehow.

A hanging shoe bag in your closet will help to keep them off the floor, or store them in their boxes stacked neatly in your closet.

When trying to rid yourself of old clothes, shoes, and boots that are only slightly used or still quite valuable, don't forget you can always have a garage sale, go to a consignment store, or sell it at an Internet auction. That way, you can tell yourself that the piece has gone to someone who will treasure it as much as you did.

Your Stuff

Now that you have cleared out the children's toys, books, clothes, and your spouse's, it is time to tackle the hard part: *Your stuff.*

One shelf at a time. One drawer at a time. One closet at a time. It might take weeks, it might take months, it might even take a year to really get your pack rat-itis under control. You may never be truly cured, but be aware of your habits and try to stay on top of things so that clutter doesn't pile up again.

It is imperative that you remove all dead plants from your environment. Don't throw them in the garbage, return them to the Earth. Don't have dried flowers anywhere, including potpourri. Dried plants drain energy. If you want fake flowers, plants, or trees, use silk.

Be aware of coins. Try not to leave coins on the floor. Keep them in a special place; don't just fling them into your jewelry box or onto your dresser. Roll them up and use them. This shows respect for money. If the universe sees you respecting money, it is more apt to send more money your way! Also, one way the spirits communicate with us is to leave coins on the floor. It is thought by some that spirits leave money, especially pennies, to indicate that they are near and watching over you. Maybe you have asked for a "sign" from a departed soul, and the mysterious appearance of coins on the floor could very well be it. However, you won't know it if you already have junk all over the place. How will you know if someone's trying to communicate with you if there are already a few pennies trapped between your nightstand and your bed?

Remove pictures of people who stress you out—old boyfriends or girlfriends, relatives, and so on. These pictures create powerful energy and will interfere with the rest of the House Magic work you are trying to do.

My partner and I were called in to do readings for a woman who kept telling me there were bad vibes in her house. She was anxious to know what to do about them. We walked in, and immediately my partner noticed an area where the energy was blocked. As I walked toward her, I felt like I was walking into a fog. The disturbance seemed to be related to the center sidewall of the room. We closed our eyes, wondering if the disturbing force was the antique cabinet, or some glassware, or the old books, but finally honed in on one tiny photograph. The woman had about twenty photographs displayed of various family and friends. We both pointed to a picture of a couple of people and said, "What is it about this picture?" The woman said the picture was of her father, and they had a turbulent relationship. Her eyes were welling up even as she looked at the picture. We told her to remove the picture for now, or at least keep it face down. The minute she put it face down, the energy clog wasn't as bad. We cleansed the room with sage, and the energy flowed once more. We blessed the picture and told her to meditate on her relationship with her father even if she couldn't work things out in person, and to send light and love to him. When she was ready, she could put the picture face out again or just remove it.

How's that bathroom looking? Is it a sea of jars and gels and hairbrushes and cosmetics? Try to keep the countertops bare. I have a hanging make-up kit that I keep on my towel rack; my medicine chest is too small for my make-up, and under my sink I store toilet paper, extra shampoo, and soap.

It is good practice too to keep the toilet lid down at all times, so you won't flush away your good fortune. This is doubly important if your bathroom is in your love or money area of your home, which will be discussed in the Feng Shui chapter. This too will solve the age-old argument about whether the toilet seat should be left up or down. The answer is, Down, with the lid shut on top.

It may not feel practical, but keeping the bathroom door closed at all times also attracts auspicious vibrations.

When you first walk into your house, do you trip over a pile of shoes? No matter how tiny your home, try to keep the main entrance clear. It should not be cluttered with shoes, coats, school bags, mail, three-day-old papers, hockey equipment, or other paraphernalia. Happy, good-fortune spirits won't be able to flow in with you if there is so much blockage. Sometimes even a little screen to create an entranceway can help channel the energy better.

Once you get the clutter cleared out of the entryway, you can experiment with what feels good in this area. How does your home look and feel when you walk through the door? Are you overwhelmed with junk all around, or is there a brief pause of space, a place to remove your shoes and put them away, room in the closet or a coat rack to hang your coat, a place to breathe before actually entering the home? It doesn't have to be big, but it has to be clear.

What is hanging on the refrigerator? What is on *top* of the fridge? Check out your bulletin boards. How old are those coupons anyway? Is all that paper pleasing to the eye, or have you gotten so used to it that you don't even see it anymore?

To see what might be clutter or not, walk into each room of your house as if it were the first time you'd ever been there. Where does your eye go? What do you see? What isn't truly necessary to be in that room at that time? Look in the ceiling corners. Clear out those cobwebs. Check those floor corners. Demolish those dust bunnies.

Remember: One room, one part of a room at a time. You are making a lifestyle change, and much like starting a healthy eating program, it's better to transform your habits slowly, one tiny step at a time. That way, you will be better able to adapt to your new way of being.

Make an effort to keep on top of dusting and vacuuming, and try not to let those little piles build up again.

✤ MIND CLUTTER

Not only do you have to physically release the past, you have to release it mentally as well. It can take years to release baggage (which is why psychiatrists get paid big bucks), so don't be upset if you find you are clinging to old loves and hurts. As long as you are taking steps to move forward in your life, your intent is showing that you are ready to transform your way of being.

The following exercises are not meant to replace any work you may be doing with a professional therapist. If you feel the need to seek professional help to cope with issues, then go and get it. You can still participate in House Magic. If you are going through a divorce or have a problem with your children or at work, pick just one challenge to focus on. Focus on how you are going to deal with one problem at a time—maybe releasing negative energy toward your ex or being firmer with the kid's bedtime rituals. Remember, one little step at a time.

The best way to release mental baggage is through meditation.

MEDITATION FOR BREATHING AND RELAXING

1 Find a quiet spot during the day, while you're taking a bath, before you go to sleep. It doesn't really matter when. If you are just beginning to practice meditation, it is best to lie on your back, no pillow, hands loosely at your side, legs down.

2 Let your mind go blank.

3 Listen to your breath.

4 Breathe in for five counts through your nose, and breathe out for five counts through your mouth.

5 Be aware of your body. Start at your toes and work your way up. Wiggle your toes when breathing in. Relax your toes by breathing out. Do the same with your feet, your ankles, your shins, and so on. Work your way up through every part of your body. Is your neck tight? Are your hands clenched? Relax them. Breathe through the tension. How is your pelvis? Your back? Your jaw? Your mouth should be slightly open, teeth apart. Check your ears, your eyebrows. Every single part of you should be relaxed. This can be one place to stop when you are first learning or are rushed for time.

6 Once you get the hang of breathing into stress release, change the counts. Find a pattern that is comfortable for you. Any time you feel a part of your body tensing, breathe it into relaxation.

7 Once your body is relaxed, let your mind wander. Go wherever it wants to take you.

8 Write down any messages you receive, no matter how strange they may be to you. You'll want to have a special workbook just for dreams, meditations, divinations, predictions, and any other metaphysical work. It can be a plain notebook; it can be a fancy art book. You can write or draw. This is your book, and you should keep it handy during meditation and while you sleep.

MEDITATION FOR RELEASING BAGGAGE

1 Do your breathing exercise until you are totally relaxed.

2 Think about white light shining down from the heavens and entering your body through your crown chakra. Imagine the white light shining through your body, filling your flesh and blood. Imagine it radiating from your fingers and toes. You are white light.

3 Whenever you meditate or do spiritual work, divination, or mediumship, you must protect yourself. The simplest way to do this is to imagine yourself in a blue bubble, as described in the introduction. No one can touch you in your blue bubble. You are safe and happy and relaxed in your blue bubble.

4 Think about the challenge facing you, the baggage you want to stop cluttering your mind.

5 Don't judge. Don't start thinking he said/she said or right/wrong. Look at the situation from an outside angle.

6 If the challenge is something that has already happened, like a divorce or a childhood hurt, let it go. If it is something that you are still working through, like a custody trial, relax. Let your mind wander around. It may work through a solution on some strange level. This is why you need your notebook right beside you when you are finished. The answer may not be clear. There may just be swirls of colors. Don't even look at the colors, look past them. Don't try to "force the story," just watch it unfold. If you get caught up in manipulating the meditation, count your breathing, listen to your breath, your blood, your heart. Check that your hands are relaxed, your jaw is loose. See the white light.

7 Whether you feel you have reached a solution or not, there comes a time where you have to come back. Forgive your ex and say good-bye. Forgive your fourth-grade teacher and say good-bye. Remember, they too are human. They too hurt and cry and feel

despair. Send them light and love. Forgive yourself. Let the negative emotions go.

8 Say good-bye to the experience. Thank the Spirit Motherfather for showing you this experience.

9 Climb out of your blue bubble and send it away until you need it again.

10 Open your eyes. Don't sit up too fast. Take a few sips of spring water to ground you. Have a small healthy snack. Make notes in your book about what you've seen, heard, felt, tasted, and smelled.

As I said, this won't remove years of baggage in one sitting. But every time you send light and love to someone who challenges you, you are opening your heart and mind to the possibility of resolution and the ability to let go and move on.

Don't try to tackle several challenges at once. Pick one at a time. Maybe several meditations on the same challenge are needed before dealing with any other. Sometimes, just dealing with one hurdle in our life releases the other ones. Everyone is different. We all grieve differently for things that might have been, we all want different things from life, we all heal and forgive at a different pace.

The point of this book is to help you be more aware of who *you* are and how to listen to your own intuition. After all, *you* are the star of your own life. There is no dress rehearsal; this is the real deal. Leave the past in the past, and devour every moment in the present as if it were your last.

Bitterness can eat us up and interfere with the work we are trying to do. We are all human. We all make mistakes. No matter how painful the situation was, it is over, and we have to live with circumstances as they are right this very moment.

You will gain strength and insight. Your confidence will grow. As your confidence in your own ability to forgive and move on grows, your energy grows stronger. When your energy is strong, your life is filled with endless possibilities. When you are strong and confident, you attract into your life people who are good for you. You attract prosperity and love, for you are loving and giving. People will want to be around you because you glow. This could be charisma, happiness, a desire to help others—whatever it is, it is yours to share. The more you share of yourself, the more the universe will reward you.

What about those tapes in your head? You know the ones: *I'm not good enough. I'm not attractive enough. I'm too shy. I'm too old. Everyone gets all the breaks but me.*

That is mind clutter too. Here again, it is a matter of breaking the cycle. And once again, it isn't going to happen overnight, so don't be hard on yourself.

Whenever you find yourself falling into a self-defeating pattern, listen to it. Why aren't you good enough? You don't know that you aren't good enough. You *are* good enough. You are just as good as anyone else. In fact you are better, because you are *you*, and there is only one you!

Every time that little voice starts harping at you, tell it that you are not that. You *are* beautiful. You *can* run that extra lap today. You *are* strong.

Positive thinking activates positive energy. When positive energy is flowing through you, anything is possible.

ᴥ BODY CLUTTER

This isn't a book about health, but a healthy body is desirable if you want to work magic. Eating properly, taking vitamins and minerals, and exercising regularly all contribute to self-confidence and provide the discipline that is necessary for gaining control over your life.

There are many books and programs and systems to explore. I wouldn't begin to tell you which one to try. I have tried many myself, some with better results than others. You have to do what is best for you, whether you are a carnivore, vegetarian, or vegan.

Make sure you get out and walk on regular basis. I adopted a large dog from the animal shelter so that I would have to leave my house in the wintertime. Winter in Canada is a challenge for me, so instead of moaning and groaning about how much I hate it, I go out and walk the dog, and try to focus on how much *he* enjoys the snow, even if I don't. Walking is healthy and gives you time to think. It can clear your mind, release tension, and build stronger bones.

You've heard all the tricks to keeping fit. Take the stairs, cut back on fat, drink at least eight glasses of water a day, and make sure that your calcium and magnesium intake is high, especially if you are a woman.

Water is important for cleansing the body, and it is great for grounding after meditation. Some people swear by dropping stones in their bottles of water for added effects. A piece of citrine can enhance abundance and creativity, for example. There are several books (see the references, page 227) that have sections on how to create your own elixirs to enhance your health, your mind, and your spirituality.

Now that you have your home, mind, and body cleansed,

you are ready to move on to further explore the world of House Magic.

Clearing the Clutter

AIR CLUTTER

Sage the room before you begin.

Ask the universe to bless the room.

ENVIRONMENTAL CLUTTER

Tackle one room at a time.

Use boxes, baskets, and files to sort and organize paper, clothes, and books.

Throw it away.

Once you've achieved order, maintain it by dusting and vacuuming regularly.

MIND CLUTTER

Practice breathing and relaxing.

Use meditation to release that baggage.

BODY CLUTTER

Eat properly.

Take vitamins and minerals.

Exercise regularly.

Drink lots of water.

3

ORGANIZERS, MESSAGE CENTERS & FAMILY ART

Usually refrigerators and bulletin boards are in the kitchen, although if you live in a dorm room or other arrangement, they may be part of your bedroom or garage or office or some other place. Wherever your refrigerators and bulletin boards are located, the same rules apply.

Following our rules for clearing out clutter, we need to be certain that our energy is flowing through and around our kitchen and not getting trapped in endless paintings, stale food, and magnets on the fridge. The same goes for bulletin boards, calendars, and family artwork.

Like everything else in your home, you want to keep the front of your fridge uncluttered. Go into your kitchen and look around. What is on your refrigerator? On the front, on the top, on the sides. . . . Take a moment and totally clear off the outside of your refrigerator. Get everything off the top of it; remove all the magnets and artwork. Wash it down until it shines.

Now that you've finished, think about your refrigerator for a minute. The refrigerator door is probably used more often than any other door in the house. So what better place to put messages of a meaningful nature than right where they will catch everyone's eye on a regular basis?

You'll need refrigerator magnets. You can use letters or maybe one of those little kits that has lots of pre-formed words. It's probably best if on the front of the fridge you write a sentence or two, or a poem or an affirmation, and then either store the unused portion of the kit in its box or stick the words to the side of the fridge. Then everyone can have easy access to words, but the extras don't clutter up the front of the fridge.

Once you have written your poem or affirmation, decide what else you want to put on your refrigerator. Maybe a picture relating to your affirmation? Are you trying to lose weight? You might want to put up a picture of how you are going to treat yourself if you lose five pounds. You could hang a picture of a nearby beach or a lake or a wood that you will visit when you reach your goal. Maybe an amusement park. Perhaps a new dress or the latest bestseller. Whatever it is, it is your tool to help you visualize. Every time you go to the fridge, you will see that lake and think about how much you want to go there. Maybe you will reach for a cold glass of water instead of a Coke, or an apple instead of that cheese-cake.

Some people say you should put a picture of someone thin and beautiful on the fridge to encourage you. Personally, I've always found that depressing. I will always be short

and I will always be me, so putting up a picture of a super-model isn't going to encourage me at all. Instead it will encourage me to grab for a large piece of cheesecake.

A picture of yourself, smiling, at any weight is probably a better idea. Especially if the picture was taken during a wonderful event that makes you smile when you think of it. Visualizing yourself happy and content will put you much further on track with balancing your mind-body connection than striving to be something that you are not.

I wouldn't put up a picture of your old self if you were thin once and gained weight when you had a baby. The average woman is meant to be round, and babies need hips and breasts to cling to. You will just torture yourself and rob yourself of those first months with your baby if you are obsessing over getting your figure back. If you have a young child, maybe a picture of a mother goddess or mother and child or something that inspires feelings of warmth and nurturing and creative growth would be a better idea.

Perhaps you really want a new car. You don't know how you're going to get it; you don't make enough money to just go out and buy one. Find a picture of one and put it on your fridge. Every time you go to the fridge, you will see that car, and you will start to think of ways that you can help yourself obtain it. Remember, the true spirit of House Magic is intent.

What is the possibility, and how are you going to achieve it?

When we are confronted with our realities, we become more creative in trying to deal with them.

Hang a bulletin board in the kitchen. I suggest that you have at least one in the kitchen for family goal setting and affirmations. Hang two or three and you can designate them for different people or different purposes. One can display items like important phone numbers, one can be especially for the children, and one dedicated to the family in general, like pictures and interesting newspaper articles. On the one I consider my "career board," I have positive reviews about my work, a letter or two, and pictures of friends I have met while traveling to conventions.

Keep your bulletin boards in brightly lit areas, and on the board, do not overlap one thing over another. Put pictures of loved ones, pets, friends, people you want to meet on your bulletin boards. Display certificates your children have earned at school or even ones you award them at home for having the cleanest room or the biggest smile. Articles relating to subjects that interest you, or something inspiring, a poem you like, maybe your yearly horoscope, current relevant business cards, and *unexpired* coupons are all good to display. Once in while you might want to put up something like tickets for a show you are going to, or an impending bill you don't want to forget but aren't certain how you will pay.

Goals

You can put goals and more affirmations on the bulletin boards. Perhaps you need to set daily goals in order to get everything accomplished that you need to. Instead of reading the paper with your morning coffee, take five minutes to jot down a few things that you need to get done that day. This can be anything from taking the kids to school to remembering to buy bread or not crying over an ex-lover. Don't overwhelm yourself; just set a few goals for the day.

If you've been having trouble getting motivated, especially if you've been ill, just had a baby, are on holiday, or are coming out a depression, you may want to consider a very simple yet effective goal list. You can divide your goals into tasks: emotional, physical, mental, and survival.

Under *Emotional,* write something kind you will do for yourself emotionally: Something like looking in the mirror, picking something you're good at, and telling yourself how you rock! "You are the best darned singer I have ever heard!"

Under *Physical,* write down one thing you will do for yourself physically: "I will walk the dog for fifteen minutes today."

Under *Mental,* pick something that will lift your spirits or undo a mental block: "I will meditate in complete and total silence with no distractions for ten minutes."

Under *Survival,* put those annoying tasks that nobody likes to do but that have to be done, because if they aren't done everything mushrooms and expands until the task is so overwhelming that it becomes a complete and total nightmare! "Do one load of laundry."

You will notice that every action I wrote down was small. This is very important. We have to be kind to ourselves, especially if we are starting new habits and rituals. If we take on too much, it can be overwhelming and become a chore, and then lifestyle changes are not possible.

You *know* much of what has to be done in your everyday life. You don't *have* to write everything down. This is just a way of keeping focused, of becoming used to goal-directed behavior. Witchcraft, wishcraft, activating auspicious vibrations into your life start with having a goal and meeting it. You have to learn the discipline of focusing and achieving your goals before any kind of witchcraft can work for you.

You set up a positive energy flow, getting the vibrations rippling across the universe and into you. Intent is the key to accomplishment.

So many people go through life thinking something is missing; they want something, but if you ask them to explain, they aren't sure what it is. If you don't know what you want, how do you know if you've got it, or more important, how do you know it is missing? Sometimes people just know there is an empty void inside of them that they can't fill. Maybe they've lost a loved one or a job, or they want children but can't have any. These are the kinds of life pains that everyone experiences to varying degrees. The thing *you* have to do is decide how you are going to fill up the gaps in your life using methods that you have control over.

Daily life functions, the little things we do to get through the day, are one way of relearning our control. Writing down that you will walk one mile with the dog that day, doing it, and then crossing it off your list is an act of meeting your goal. Setting out to do something and then completing it with success gives us more confidence to go on and meet the bigger challenges.

Post your daily list on your bulletin board. And don't forget to cross things off as you accomplish them. That's the best thing about lists: meeting your goals.

You can then make other lists as well. Weekly, monthly, and life path. You can change your lists as often as you want, but don't forget: It is no good to make lists if you don't look at them.

✧ CALENDARS

Don't forget to keep a calendar. You can put one on the bulletin board, or hang it somewhere else. I tend to have several calendars in different rooms. You don't have to mark all your calendars for special events; pick one and stay with it. The kitchen calendar is probably the best for that. You can use stickers to mark things like doctor's appointments and moon cycles.

I always carry an astrological day timer in my briefcase so that I know where the moon is and other interesting things as I go about my day. If the moon is in Pisces, I know I'll be feeling more sentimental and emotional, maybe daydreaming a lot.

✧ CHILDREN'S ART

If you have children, you might want to put up one of their paintings or two. But not too many. What worked for me when my children were young was to designate a wall in the

kitchen for their artwork instead of the fridge or a bulletin board. It was like our own personal art gallery for a couple of years. Maybe you're a Virgo and don't like the idea of hand-painted splotches hanging in your kitchen. I can't tell you what to do, but I do know that it means the world to the kids if they see their artwork hanging up in a special place. You will have many years later to hang those collectors' plates and pieces of modern art. For now, just relax and enjoy the bright creative flow that children bring into our lives. Their enthusiasm vibrates from their creativity, and displaying their artwork adds positive vibrations into our homes.

Every now and again—once a month or so—walk into the kitchen as if you've never been there before. How are those bulletin boards looking? Is everything on there still relevant? Is the calendar turned to the correct month or day? Is there anything you should take down?

If we operate on the theory that all the best parties end up in the kitchen, then you want your space to be able to handle the excited energy of your friends and give them something pleasant to look at, instead of just outdated coupons and broken fruit magnets. Keep your fridge, calendars, and bulletin boards neat and your kitchen energy will flow much better, whether it's just for you alone or for your family.

Organizers, Message Centers & Family Art

THE REFRIGERATOR

Keep your kitchen free of clutter.

Clear off the top and sides of your refrigerator.

Put affirmations, or an inspiring picture or poem, on your refrigerator.

BULLETIN BOARDS

Use bulletin boards for family lists, goals, and affirmations.

Organize your goals into manageable lists.

Use your lists and check items off as you accomplish them.

Put up a couple of snapshots from happy events.

CALENDARS

Keep a current calendar in view with all your appointments and goal dates.

CHILDREN'S ARTWORK

Create an art gallery of your children's work.

4

ASTROLOGY

Nearly everyone is familiar with the concepts of astrology, the zodiac, and the twelve sun signs. If someone asks you what sign you are, chances are you know the sign's name, its symbol, and a key word or phrase describing it. Taurus the Bull is stubborn, Aquarius the Water Bearer is lofty, Sagittarius the Archer likes to travel, and so on. You might be surprised to learn that many factors influence your chart, which is why you can know two people of the same sign who are total opposites.

✦ SUN, MOON, AND RISING SIGNS

There is more to astrology than just knowing your sun sign. In addition to our sun signs, we are affected very strongly by our moon signs and our rising signs. If you don't know your moon and rising signs, you can find them at one of the on-line astrology sites, look them up in an ephemeris—a book that details exactly where the planets were at your moment of birth—go to an astrologer, or learn how to cast your own chart.

Your sun sign reveals the masculine traits of your personality. It is the real you, the you your friends and family know. Your sun sign reflects your ambitions, the way you meet challenges, the career path you are suited for, and the lifestyle that appeals to you.

Your moon sign reveals the feminine side of your personality. This is your secret self, your intuitive sense, the way you think and perceive things, your disposition and moods. Someone with a Cancer moon may be moody.

Your ascendant or rising sign is the sign that was rising over the horizon when you were born. Most of the time, it is different from your sun sign. This sign reveals how you present yourself to others. Your rising sign is what people see when they first meet you, your public face or "mask." Someone with Leo rising may attract a lot of attention when they enter a room because of their flamboyant style of dress or their "mane" of hair. Someone with Gemini rising may be friendly and talkative.

How you love, how you solve problems, how you plan, what sort of environment soothes you or agitates you are all reflected in the planets and their placement in your personal chart. You may find you are more like your moon sign than your sun sign, especially as you get older. Or you may find you reflect a blend of styles; this too is because of planetary influences. There is no right or wrong way to choose if you use your intuition.

Every planet affects a person differently, and the planets are all in different places in every person's astrological birth chart. Someone could be an Aquarius with a Gemini moon and Leo rising, which would give them a more outgoing and carefree personality than an Aquarian with a Cancer moon and Capricorn rising, who would be more of a cautious, careful, homebody type. Where the planets are at your time of birth and on any given day influence who you are and how you act. If you can understand your sun sign, your moon sign, and your rising sign, you will have a good grasp of who you are.

Sometimes, too, if we are aware of other people's strengths and weaknesses or likes or dislikes as represented by their astrological signs, we can interact with those people more easily. A sign that is associated with neatness and order, like Virgo, will be unhappy living with a bunch of relaxed roommates. Some people are more timid than others; some, such as Capricorn, like privacy; while others, like Sagittarius, enjoy a Grand Central Station atmosphere. Some, like Aquarius, are drawn to bright colors and modern furniture, while Cancers prefer soothing shades and comfortable antiques.

The different signs are attracted to and affected by different plants, colors, and stones. Some of the more popular ideas about these relationships and how they can enhance your life are covered in this chapter and elsewhere in this book. (See chapters 7, 8, and 9, on plants, gemstones, and colors.)

When you're practicing House Magic, you can activate positive energy by being aware of the element—fire, water, air, or earth—that is represented by your sign and by incorporating the plants, colors, and gemstones that relate to it. You can come up with decorating ideas that will please everyone in your household by considering the sun signs of your children, spouse, or housemates, and adding little flourishes that appeal to those signs.

You will find that in many books, this one included, there are differing opinions on what plants, colors, and stones go with which sign. I used several systems from different sources to compile the information presented here.

A Leo might be naturally drawn to warm, "sunny" colors, since Leo is a fire sign ruled by the sun. But she could also be drawn to purple because of its regal, royal implications; one of Leo's favorite plants is lavender. Maybe he loves the color red. After all, one of their ruling stones is ruby, and we all know how beautiful Dorothy's ruby slippers were! What Leo wouldn't want a pair of those?

You can use colors to bring out a sense of happiness or contentment in your surroundings, to really make your home feel like your own, where you can feel true to yourself and at

the same time activate auspicious energy. Again, if you are a Leo, you probably wouldn't want to paint a whole room red, for that would bring out too much of the fire (aggression, sexual energy) in your personality. Maybe just an accent of red, like a throw pillow in a pale yellow room, would be better.

The gemstones listed rule the sign and/or activate vibrations necessary to enhance or alleviate certain aspects of the sign. All gemstones are useful with all signs, but some may help certain signs more than others because of the vibrations the stones give off. Moonstones are good for dream work and psychic abilities, especially for Pisceans and Cancers who are naturally psychic. But any sign can benefit from moonstones.

Signs that are naturally "flighty," like Aquarius or Sagittarius, can benefit from the grounding effects of a stone like hematite, but it will work for anyone. Turquoise can provide healing and protection for those sometimes accident-prone Sagittarius and Aries.

The information here is offered as guidelines to enhance the natural abilities of a sign. The very best way to choose what you need is to see what you are naturally drawn to and find out a bit about it. Sometimes we are drawn to what we are missing in our lives, so even if you are attracted by a stone that isn't listed as "your stone," listen to your gut feeling. There just might be a reason for it.

Many stones overlap in their uses. Sometimes there are reasons why one stone will work better for "healing" than another. We don't have room here to explain all the various details of the different crystals, gemstones, and minerals, but *Love Is in the Earth* is a good book that describes each stone's qualities in more detail.

We continue this chapter with an explanation of the four elements, then offer a quick overview of each sign, its ruling planet, and its auspicious plants, colors, and stones. Include some of these items in your home environment and be ready for the positive changes they will invite! (For more details on sign preferences and needs, pick up a good astrology book. Several are listed in the References.)

↦ THE FOUR ELEMENTS

The twelve signs of the zodiac are governed by four elements: fire, water, air, and earth. I like to compare the elements of the zodiac to the four suits of a traditional tarot card deck. The Minor Arcana set of cards used in tarot is similar to a regular playing card deck. There are four suits—wands, cups, swords, and pentacles—each of which is related to one of the four elements.

In a tarot deck, the suit of wands represents the fire sign energies: aggression, sexual energy, travel, tenacity, creativity, tempers that flare up and burn out quickly. The suit of cups represents the water sign energies: heightened emotions, passion, love, psychic energy, creativity, moodiness. The suit of swords represents air sign energies: intellect, honesty, justice, impatience, mental energy, stress, a sharp tongue. The suit of pentacles or coins represents the earth sign energies: groundedness, stability, reliability, stubbornness, business acumen, financial skills, and sometimes spiritualism.

The Fire Signs

Fire signs—Aries, Leo, Sagittarius—reflect masculinity, fiery energy, motivation, ambition, sexual energy, drive, creative growth, enthusiasm, movement, and travel. They correspond to the suit of wands in the tarot.

Courageous, bold, tenacious and proud,
Fire signs are easy to spot in a crowd.
Flowing manes tossing, eyes bright with ideas,
Their infectious enthusiasm draws everyone near!

They speak of adventure in faraway places,
Of kings and queens and strange foreign graces.

They'll hop in a car or a plane in a flash,
Usually not bothering to count their cash!

Fire signs burn bright with the spark of new life;
Inspirational ideas keep them up half the night!

A fire sign's passion means you've found a good
  friend.
If you can keep up, they'll be there 'til the end!

The Water Signs

Water signs—Cancer, Scorpio, Pisces—are ruled by love,
passion, emotions, and creativity. They are maternal, psychic, secretive, and live in a fantasy world. They are the suit
of cups in a tarot deck.

Compassionate, nurturing, emotional, sensitive,
Water signs are the romantic intuitive.
Gaze into their dreamy, benevolent eyes
And witness the presence of countless past lives.

They are happy at home in their own cozy shell.
Reading, sewing, and movies amuse them quite well.
They listen to loved ones with a tolerant ear,
They cherish their lovers more when they're near.

Water signs are passionate, creative, and deep.
Dreams cling to their minds after waking from sleep.
A water sign's passion means you've found a good
   friend.
If you like to dream big, they'll be yours 'til the end!

The Air Signs

Air signs—Gemini, Libra, Aquarius—ruled by the suit of swords, are governed by intellect, logic, a sense of honor, balance, and fair play. Masculine energy can cause them to be cutting, daring, and impulsive.

Logical, analytical, intellectual, bold,
Air signs can whirl by or stop you dead cold.
Sarcastic remarks can flit from their tongue,
Whether joking or serious, you'd just better succumb.

They're ahead in their thoughts, in two different
   spaces.
Air signs love to travel, to explore strange new places.
They'll hop on a plane or a boat in a flash
Usually without any regard for their cash.

Air signs are the wind in the sails of life.
They'll keep your brain churning for half of the night.

An air sign's honesty means you've found a good
    friend,
If you can stand their analyses, they'll be there 'til the
    end.

The Earth Signs

Earth signs—Taurus, Virgo, Capricorn—are ruled by the suit
of pentacles. They are feminine, nurturing, stable, reliable,
and demanding of the best that money can buy. They aren't
usually afraid to work for their cash.

Generous, dependable, practical, and loyal,
Earth signs are solid, like a handful of rich soil!
They are the ones firmly standing in line
Organizing their wallets to preserve precious time.

They know where their money goes every step of the
    way
And will pamper themselves with a treat on payday.
They love classic clothes, classic books, classic shows.
Earth signs have gardens with no weeds and straight
    rows!

Earth signs love travel, there is so much to see!
They'll be certain to stick to their itinerary.

An earth sign's loyalty means you've found a good
   friend,
If you pamper them occasionally, they'll be there 'til
   the end.

Aries March 21–April 20

   ELEMENT Fire

   RULING PLANET Mars

   SYMBOL The Ram

   PRIMARY MODE Intuition

   KEY PHRASE I Am

   LIFE LESSON Try to follow projects through to the end.

With exuberant energy, Aries bravely initiates the most ambitious of adventures. Impulsiveness can lead to physical ac-
cidents when they leap from mountaintop to mountaintop.
Intensely focused on her goal, Aries is unmindful of the
rocks tumbling down onto those who are trying to keep
pace. Aries the Ram is the first sign of the zodiac and is often
referred to as a child. They are playful, adventurous people

who thrive on new experiences and travel. Aries doesn't sit still for long and is forever forging new paths. They like to be the leaders in group situations and aren't afraid to go first. Sometimes they are so busy rushing from here to there that they can be accident-prone. The passionate fire of Aries burns brightest with hard work and competition.

Ruled by fire, Arians are attracted to bright, vibrant colors. Reds and oranges accenting browns and greens would make the Ram feel right at home. Furniture shouldn't be too fussy, as the Ram will always be jumping up and puttering with something. Even the adult Aries likes to have toys, often relating to a hobby or special interest. Big screen TVs, fancy stereos, video games, and computers will be found in an Aries home. Aries have to be the first on the block with any new gadget or appliance. If you want to bring a housewarming present for an Aries, try new books, especially adventure novels and biographies of pioneers in the various arts, new clothes, new wines, something personalized, or something related to one of their sporty hobbies. Be certain to wrap that present in an interesting way.

PLANTS Poppies, thistles, ferns, and tiger lilies

COLORS Red, black, and white

STONES Ruby *promotes assertiveness*

Diamond *increases self-confidence*

Emerald *enhances communication skills*

Amethyst *brings healing, relieves headaches, soothes impatience*

Taurus April 21–May 21

ELEMENT Earth

RULING PLANET Venus

SYMBOL The Bull

PRIMARY MODE Sensation

KEY PHRASE I Have

LIFE LESSON Learn to move on.

Taurus the Bull has a reputation for being the most stubborn sign of the zodiac. Honest and practical Taurus will persevere long after others have given in. They love to curl up with a romantic book in bed or on a special reading couch, surrounded by luxurious satins and silks, overstuffed pillows, with rich food like chocolate to nibble on. Chronic self-pampering can lead to laziness, weight concerns, or finding themselves stuck in a rut. Responsible and reliable Taurus is a loyal friend who usually has money squirreled away for a rainy day. Once a Taurus has made up her mind, there is no budging her. They are kind, considerate people, sometimes shy and deeply romantic. Lovers of nature, harmony, and all living things, they are creative and nurturing. They are the most loyal of friends, even if they do drive you insane while you are waiting for them to make up their minds.

Ruled by Venus, Taurus is very sensual. They crave that all their senses be stimulated by sight, scent, touch, taste and sound. They prefer real flowers to fake ones, the best chocolates, the finest wines, luxurious fabrics. Taurus appreciates the fine things in life. Taurus is one of the more materialistic signs of the zodiac; even if he doesn't have much money, he demands top quality. They are creatures of habit, and once they have decided where to put their furniture and knick-knacks, it will take a lot of convincing to get them to move them. They don't like change of any kind. Don't come barging in expecting to whisk a Taurus off somewhere; she needs time to deliberate over the details and decide what to wear.

They like their homes to be orderly and tend to buy luxurious yet comfortable furniture that will increase in value over time. Gifts for a Taurus are easy to figure out: If it is costly, and fit for a king or queen, your Taurus will love it.

PLANTS Daisy, dandelion, lily, mallow

COLORS Pastel shades, blue, deep green

STONES Topaz *brings love and success*

Rose quartz *is soothing, inspires imagination, peace*

Emerald *promotes learning, self-confidence, communication*

Lapis lazuli *enhances speech, hearing, writing, insight*

Gemini May 22–June 21

ELEMENT Air

RULING PLANET Mercury

SYMBOL The Twins

PRIMARY MODE Thought

KEY PHRASE I Communicate

LIFE LESSON Try to read one book at a time . . . just once!

Lively, articulate Gemini is always on the go, flitting from subject to subject, book to book, learning just enough to satisfy their active, curious minds before bouncing on. A Gemini confined by job or inability to travel is a sad, frustrated creature. Young at heart, these high-strung versatile personalities can be fickle but they are always entertaining!

There is no one quite like a Gemini. This Peter Pan of the zodiac is in constant movement, bursting with ideas and ready to tell you all about everything at the drop of a hat. They are so curious that they will constantly interrupt you with questions and will always be reading a book or two or three. Sometimes their nervous energy can be disruptive to calmer signs, because Gemini seldom sits still for long.

They are ruled by Mercury, the planet of communication, which means they are probably on the phone or in chat rooms a great deal. Their sense of fun, natural charm, intuitive sense, and compassion makes them lively guests and friends, although they can be prone to gossip, fickleness, and plain old manipulation. Their gift of gab makes them excellent salespeople.

A Gemini will have a home that reflects her myriad interests, lots of technological equipment, the latest gadgets, and rooms with minimal furniture so that she can dash around on tangents without slamming into things. They enjoy having company.

PLANTS	Tansy, yarrow, privet, orchids, hybrids
COLORS	Yellow, orange, light green
STONES	Citrine *enhances communication*
	Amber *encourages mental clarity, calms nervous stomach, mood swings*
	Tourmaline *soothes anxiety; healing, grounding*

Cancer June 22–July 22

ELEMENT Water

RULING PLANET The Moon

SYMBOL The Crab

PRIMARY MODE Feeling

KEY PHRASE I Feel

LIFE LESSON Sometimes you just have to let go!

Cancer is a homebody who prefers hanging around the backyard barbecue to eating out in a restaurant. Cancer likes nothing more than to provide for and pamper family members. Even if Cancer has a demanding career, he will still find time to cook or add little touches around the house to show that he cares. Cancer is very sensitive and tends to retreat if times are tough or if she has been slighted in some way.

Cancers have incredible memories and will remember both the good times and the bad, long after most others have forgotten.

Ruled by the Moon, Cancers are very intuitive, secretive, and can work well with dreams. They are perhaps one of the most naturally psychic signs of the zodiac. Their compassion makes them good friends, and their strong gut feelings make them excellent salespeople.

They almost always have food in the fridge and are usually good cooks. They tend to like having a lot of pillows and blankets around. They worry a lot, especially about their family members. Sometimes they are too clingy and overprotective. They can cling to unhappy relationships out of fear of being left alone, which can exacerbate their natural tendency to worry, leading to stomach problems and mental upset.

Antiques appeal to their sense of nostalgia, and they like to collect and hoard articles of value.

PLANTS   Water lilies, rushes, lotus, moonwort, almond

COLORS   Pale colors, cream, white, silver

STONES Moonstone *eases stress, anxiety, moodiness, relieves stomachaches*

Pearl *soothes sadness and depression, lessens loneliness, strengthens bones*

Peridot *encourages optimism, inner strength*

Leo July 23–August 23

ELEMENT Fire

RULING PLANET The Sun

SYMBOL The Lion

PRIMARY MODE Intuition

KEY PHRASE I Create

LIFE LESSON Focus on other people's desires and opinions once in a while.

When Leo enters the room, you know it. They may be quiet or loud, but their countenance demands attention. Leos often have interesting hair, and will touch it, toss it, or check it in the mirror. They are usually happy, pleasant people who like excitement. Natural leaders, they are often found at the heads of organizations, large and small.

Ruled by the sun, they are warm, friendly, and compassionate. They thrive on entertaining in their homes and will treat their guests with respect and top-notch hospitality. Sometimes their desire for adoration can lead to arrogance, for Leo has to be king wherever he goes. Some signs might find the Leo a bit too high maintenance, as Leos need a lot of praise or at least reassurance that they are the best.

Beware a frustrated Leo denied what she desires! She will roar loudly, but her temper will blow over quickly with a bit of reassurance and a gentle touch.

Leo rules the roost in the home. No matter what level of income, there is a touch of elegance and regality. Leo loves comfort, so expect puffy pillows and luxurious bedspreads, plush couches and elegant curtains. Leos love mirrors, so if there's a Leo in your household, be certain the mirrors are set in the most auspicious places such as on a wall beside the door so they can check their hair before they leave the house. Leo expects the best, so hardcover books, the latest fashions, and furnishings will go far. If you are giving a gift, be certain it is wrapped with lavish care.

PLANTS   Sunflower, laurel, chamomile, lavender

COLORS   Yellow, orange, ochre

STONES	Tiger's eye *promotes vitality*
	Ruby *increases strength and courage*
	Milky yellow amber *enhances clarity and confidence*
	Yellow topaz *restores inner calm, eases stress*

Virgo August 24 –September 22

ELEMENT Earth

RULING PLANET Mercury

SYMBOL The Virgin

PRIMARY MODE Sensation, Thought

KEY PHRASE I Serve

LIFE LESSON Look in the mirror and love who you see.

Virgo the Virgin desires order in the home. This is a sign of serving others, and Virgo always tries to please. They are often witty and charming people with a tendency toward nervousness, and, of course, the legendary Virgo scathing criticism. Virgo knows what's best for everyone and won't worry twice about letting others know what's on their minds. The thing to remember about Virgo is that the person he is most critical of is himself.

Ruled by the planet Mercury, they are communicators. They constantly seek self-improvement and will read and take courses to do so. They are often workaholics, worrying about providing the best for their loved ones.

Virgo homes are orderly and clean, even if they don't think so. They probably have a wide variety of fancy soaps and toiletries, as they are fussy about their personal hygiene and grooming. As an earth sign, they love plants, gardening, and small animals.

Before they will sit down to read or watch TV, everything must be in its place. They would enjoy items that keep everything in order, such as filing systems, jewelry boxes, home improvement gadgets, and spice racks.

PLANTS	Narcissus, vervain, herbs, winter green, sage, privet
COLORS	Yellow-green, brown, cream, blue, silver, indigo, dark violet
STONE	Amethyst *encourages mental peace, releases addictions*
	Carnelian *calms, restores confidence, soothes stomach aches, bad dreams*
	Pyrite *enhances self-confidence, concentration, and vitality*

Libra September 23–October 22

> **ELEMENT** Air
>
> **RULING PLANET** Venus
>
> **SYMBOL** The Scales
>
> **PRIMARY MODE** Thought, Sensation
>
> **KEY PHRASE** I Weigh
>
> **LIFE LESSON** Life isn't always fair; relax and enjoy the moment.

Libras are friendly, lively people who can be chatterboxes. They have wonderful senses of humor and are usually up on the latest trends. They try to be fair minded about everything, and often truly see both sides to a situation, which renders it hard for them either to make a decision or to side with one or the other in an argument. Ever the intellectual diplomat, Libra is so busy balancing the scales of justice that he often appears cold and aloof. Though they may not admit it, Libras love to argue just for the sake of arguing.

Libras make loyal friends but have a tendency to put people on pedestals, especially people who have captured their hearts, and then become bitterly disillusioned when their idol is revealed as human after all. It can be very hard to live up to the Libran ideal. Charming Libra needs to love and will spend a great deal of time socializing in order to avoid what they truly fear, being alone.

Libras love luxurious items and adore being pampered. They spend a lot of time sitting around reading or listening to music. Good gifts for Libras include flowers, cards, artwork, coffee table books, and clothes. They enjoy reading and learning about historical events, as this reminds them that the scales of justice always swing back.

PLANTS   Pansy, primrose, violet, strawberry, aloe, myrtle, rose

COLORS   Primary colors, shocking pink, night blue, purple

STONES   Opal *energizes, enhances judgment*

Jade *represents courage, compassion, decisions, loyalty*

Scorpio October 23–November 21

ELEMENT Water

RULING PLANET Pluto

SYMBOL The Scorpion

Astrology 97

PRIMARY MODE Feeling

KEY PHRASE I Control

LIFE LESSON Open up, you have a lot to share!

Scorpios are mysterious, tenacious, and magnetic. If a Scorpio wants your attention, he'll get it with his penetrating stare or his intense personality. Scorpios are often dynamic, charismatic people who demonstrate a lot of compassion. They are also secretive and jealous. If you cross them, they will never forget it, and they will be certain you don't either. Scorpios will track you down to the ends of the earth, either for love or for revenge.

Tireless, they will hunt down a mystery or search for clues long after most people have given up. If they've set their sight on something, they will more likely than not get it, especially if they are in tune with their intuition or delving in dream work.

Often, Scorpios are drawn to the dark side of fantasy life and the occult. They don't reveal what they are thinking about, but their minds are always going, always analyzing, always trying to find an alternative way to achieve their goals.

They like their homes to be self-contained and comfortable, and they guard their territory and possessions. They are usually neat people, enjoying order. Always ask a Scorpio for permission before you touch anything! They are protective of their children and are empathetic with sick people. Since they are competitive and love to decipher mysteries, they enjoy puzzles, detective novels, skill-testing games, and archeological treasures.

PLANTS   Root vegetables, black poppy, hemlock

COLORS   Black, blood red, burgundy, charcoal gray

STONES   Ruby *increases courage*
Garnet *balances sexual drive*
Carnelian *provides grounding, warmth*
Black pearl *enhances calm and solace*

Sagittarius   November 22–December 21

ELEMENT Fire

RULING PLANET Jupiter

SYMBOL The Archer

PRIMARY MODE Intuition

KEY PHRASE I Philosophize

LIFE LESSON Stop and enjoy the physical presence of those who love you!

Astrology   ✧ 99

MOUNT VERNON CITY LIBRARY

Sagittarians are adventurous, fun-loving people who love to travel. They are always on the move, looking for new experiences. They may have more than one home and go wherever their fancy takes them. They are passionate people and good conversationalists. Sometimes they tend to be preachy, giving opinions from their high horse, and they often don't notice that they are being overbearing. They are natural teachers, gifted speakers, great at dealing with people.

They are very much into philosophy and trying to understand various ways that people tick. This tends to make them avid readers.

Ruled by Jupiter, the planet of expansion, they are always pushing the limits, galloping off to discover what is next on the horizon.

Being impulsive, they will whisk you off to a party or on an adventure at the drop of a hat. They are very social, and you will find them flirting and telling jokes at parties.

Motivated, they can be quite tenacious, especially when it comes to their careers. Money doesn't mean that much to them, but they can spend it without thinking twice, often on gifts and gadgets for loved ones. They enjoy going to and having parties and love to indulge in food and drink. Good gifts include books on philosophy or travel; they love lottery tickets and other forms of speculation. They enjoy comfort and like to have gadgets that make life easier, as they don't have time to be fussy when they are racing off to their next grand adventure.

PLANTS Asparagus, chestnuts, soybeans, rush, oak, fig, hyssop

COLORS Denim blue, royal blue, purple, white, beige, bronze

STONES Turquoise *protects against catastrophe*

Amethyst *promotes mental peace, calming, healing*

Citrine *aligns higher and lower selves*

Capricorn December 22–January 20

ELEMENT Earth

RULING PLANET Saturn

SYMBOL The Goat

PRIMARY MODE Sensation

KEY PHRASE I Master

LIFE LESSON We all have to die some day; first, live!

Capricorns are known for having the driest wits in the zodiac. They are careful-minded people with large doses of pessimism. They consider facts carefully before taking action. They are good providers and are house proud, enjoying comfortable yet beautiful furnishings.

Capricorns are not afraid of hard work, especially if it means furnishing their homes with good quality furniture and buying practical well-made clothing that will last for years.

It can be hard to get to know a Capricorn, as they are guarded with their emotions because they are so shy. Sometimes they come off as being cold when in fact they are just being cautious. They are very sensitive and have a fear of rejection. Being natural pessimists, they just know that something bad is going to happen.

They are often drawn to dark fantasy and escapist stories. They view the world with a sense of doom and gloom, which can sometimes be hard for others to take.

They thrive on structure and routine, and their home lives are orderly. Family and relatives and business associates are the most likely to be invited over for fine dining, as they enjoy entertaining those they have opened up to. They often belong to exclusive clubs.

Capricorns enjoy high-quality gifts, diamonds, antiques,

and anything to do with their business. They enjoy fantasy and horror novels. Since they always like to look their best, traditional clothing also makes a good gift, if you know their exact size. They are often workaholics and have to be reminded to relax once in a while. They have a strong sense of duty and responsibility, and they hate surprises.

PLANTS Hemlock, black poppy, burdock root, yew, ash, hemp, weeping willow

COLORS Brown, orange, green, black, gray, indigo, violet

STONES Diamond *enhances self-confidence, heightens ambition*

Falcon's eye *increases visionary power, intuition*

White sapphire *promotes discipline*

Aquarius January 21–February 19

ELEMENT Air

RULING PLANET Uranus

SYMBOL The Water Bearer

PRIMARY MODE Thought

KEY PHRASE I Know

LIFE LESSON Think twice before giving your opinion!

Aquarius, the Water Bearer, has friends from all walks of life. Curious and friendly, they will befriend people just to find out what makes those people tick. Even though they have loads of acquaintances, they tend to have only a handful of people whom they consider close friends. They are very loyal despite their flirtatious and impulsive natures.

They are constantly pushing the boundaries and have a strong rebellious streak, especially against the rules of society. They tend to see the big picture and don't like to get caught up in the day-to-day problems that plague most people.

They can be opinionated, since they are good problem solvers, can be very stubborn in their views. They can be too blunt for some of the more sensitive signs, since they tend to call things as they see them and consider the repercussions later.

Though they will tell others what to do, they resent being told themselves. Uranus, the planet of sudden change, can make them appear flighty to the more traditional signs, yet to an Aquarian, everything they do has an underlying sense of logic. They analyze everything and can spend as much time contemplating the secrets of the universe as where the neighbor is going so early in the morning.

They are usually on the cutting edge of trends and love the latest in technology. Computers, stereos, books on science fiction and biographies, gadgets, and anything unusual make good presents for Aquarius. They can be found in chat rooms and probably belong to several clubs and organizations. The more things they can find to do for free, the better. Their homes can range from total chaos to complete order. They are caring parents and honest, loyal friends.

PLANTS Dandelions, resins, frankincense, myrrh, olive, aspen

COLORS Electric blue, silver gray, fluorescent colors, violet, light yellow

STONES Amazonite *promotes communication*

Aquamarine *releases emotions, combats depression*

Hematite *grounds Uranian influences*

Amber *calms restlessness, mood swings*

Pisces February 20–March 20

ELEMENT Water

RULING PLANET Neptune

SYMBOL The Fish

PRIMARY MODE Feeling

KEY PHRASE I Believe

LIFE LESSON Drag yourself out of the dream pool and enjoy the moment!

Pisces, the Fish, is a dreamer. They are great at foreseeing what needs to be done and problem solving, often working from a heightened sense of intuition. They are nostalgic and sentimental and can be very emotional. They often seem on the verge of tears, whether it is because they are happy or sad. They can be downright moody and appear wishy-washy. Don't forget that the symbol for Pisces is two fish swimming in opposite directions, and often, that is how these beguiling and enchanting people appear to the rest of us. Sometimes it is hard to get them to live in the real world.

You can usually tell a Pisces by their unusual and dreamy eyes. They spend a lot of time living far in the future or in another world all together.

Pisces is very creative in the arts and in business. They are caring, compassionate people who cherish their friends and family. They usually do very well in business, especially if they have a moon or rising sign that gets them motivated. Pisces can usually get anyone to do anything for them.

Since they spend so much time in the dream world, Pisces tend to run an unstructured household. They often lose track of time, so they need clocks and watches. Their homes can range from utter chaos to neatness. They need space for privacy. Romantic and very sensual, they love poetry, music, art, candles, incense, fine wines, mystical artifacts, and personalized objects.

PLANTS   Mosses, ferns, seaweed

COLORS   Mauve, purple, aquamarine, violet, light green, blue, sea green

STONES   White opal *enhances awareness of illusion*

Jade *calms fears*

Pearls *soothes*

Amethyst *helps fight addictions*

Astrology

SUN, MOON, AND RISING SIGNS

We are often recognized by our sun signs, yet we are far more complex than that. Get to know your moon sign (your secret side) and your rising sign (the mask you wear for others) for a more complete picture.

Learn what your ruling planet is and read up on how it affects you.

Discover what plants, colors, and stones, can enhance the strengths of your sign and try to incorporate them into your living space.

THE FOUR ELEMENTS

The signs of the zodiac are categorized into four elements: fire, water, air, and earth. Learn the keywords for each element so that you can understand yourself and your friends better.

THE TWELVE SUN SIGNS

Each sign of the zodiac has its own quirks and preferences. Learning more about what motivates and inspires us can help us to lead more productive lives. Discovering which plants, stones, and colors enhance our environment will help you to bring in more positive energy so that you can be successful at creating House Magic.

5

FENG SHUI

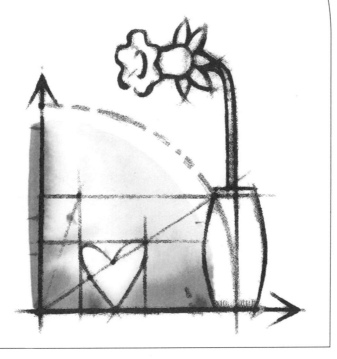

The Chinese science of Feng Shui has been in existence for thousands of years. You may have noticed it booming in popularity recently, with courses popping up, shelves of books expanding, people promoting it on talk shows, and even mainstream department stores selling items from wind chimes to dragons to Chinese coins to Feng Shui kits for attracting good luck into your home.

Feng Shui is a system of balance and harmony that incorporates the laws of nature and our place in it. If we can be in harmony with our environment, we attract positive energy flow and good luck—auspicious energy. The positive energy you create by being aware of how to organize your living space is called *chi* and is referred to as "dragon's breath." If you can create good *chi* in your home, you will have good luck, prosperity, good health, peace, and enjoyment of life.

Feng Shui practices begin with the exterior of the house, the way it faces, what is around it, the neighborhood, other houses and their yards, then it works inward, to individual rooms, and then to the smallest detail, such as pictures on the walls and knick-knacks. The idea is to create energy flow in harmony with nature so that we are part of nature, instead of invading it.

The Compass Method

There are several versions of Feng Shui; traditional practitioners swear by the "compass method." This requires the use of a special compass and strict adherence both to the big picture, starting with the direction your house is facing, and to the tiniest detail, such as the way an ornament on your shelf is facing. In addition, the material (element) of which something is made has importance; each element—wood, fire, earth, metal, water—represents characteristics in itself and also interacts with other elements.

I have found the compass method to be a rigid and disciplined system, and, quite frankly, daunting with so much to learn and pay attention to. Since many of us cannot afford to custom-build our homes to exact specifications and don't have the time or inclination to learn the intricacies of such a complex system, I provide here only a taste of some of the more practical methods of building an auspicious energy flow.

Even with a simplified version of the compass system, Feng Shui relies heavily on the use of direction; you might want to buy a compass so that you can be aware of where your north, south, east, and west are located. One way of finding the directions is to stand in the middle of the room with a compass and find north. Then look at the grid that appears later in this chapter and determine where everything is.

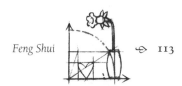

Feng Shui

The Pa Kua Method

In North America, we lean toward a version of Feng Shui called the *Pa Kua* or *Ba Gua,* which divides the home into nine sections and which is much easier to understand. Some traditionalists say that this version has no value if you don't use the compass directions, but in our lives of limited time and maximum stress, this simpler version may be better than not trying Feng Shui at all. You can use the grid that appears later in this chapter to find the nine "life sections" or "corners" in your home, then use your compass for the optimum effect. You will find, for example, that your love corner is in the southwest section of your home.

Once you have divided your home into its nine sections, you can then break down each room in the house into nine sections as well. Then you can start to make those dead corners come alive and make sure your mirrors are facing the right way!

When you begin to introduce Feng Shui into your home, it is best to start slowly. Start small—one room, one corner at a time. Even the most ardent Feng Shui counselors will advise you to start one step at a time, being very aware that every action brings a reaction. You may become overwhelmed if you attempt to Feng Shui your entire home at once.

The foundation of Feng Shui is balance, harmony, working

in synch with the natural rhythms of the environment. It is considered a science, not a magical system. It can take years to master. In this book, I can give only the smallest tidbits of information about using the principles of Feng Shui in your own House Magic. If you'd like to learn more, you will find at the library and bookstore many excellent books that go into great detail about the various ways to Feng Shui your home. (Several are listed in the References section.) Also, you can hire people who specialize in Feng Shui to analyze your home or office.

✎ THE FIVE ELEMENTS

The whole concept of Feng Shui is built on harmonizing the elements. Here is just a brief rundown on what they mean. You will notice they are similar to the elements in Western astrology, with air represented by metal in Feng Shui. Feng Shui uses a fifth element—wood— that is not used in Western astrology. It helps us to be aware of the similarities between the two systems and to remember what each element represents.

WOOD Growth, nurturing, versatility

FIRE Happiness, honor, aggression

EARTH Instinct, wisdom

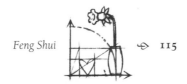

METAL Communication, justice

WATER Creativity, emotions

⟜ THE COLORS

Colors mean much the same in Feng Shui as they do in any of the other disciplines. To activate more of the energy associated with a given color, you can use candles, cushions, curtains, and so on. To activate a corner better, use the corresponding color for that corner, such as red for the love corner.

BLACK Mood, perception. Do not use too much black, as this can be draining.

BLUE Water and heaven

BROWN Nurturing

GOLD Strength, royal

GREEN Health, growth, peace, harmony

GREY Communication

PINK Love, romance

PURPLE Spiritual guidance

RED Attraction, warmth, strength, happiness. Use red sparingly, as it can stimulate arguments.

YELLOW Energy, life

WHITE Peace, purity

↭ THE NINE SECTIONS

The principle of the nine sections applies both to the house as a total entity and to individual rooms. An easy way to begin incorporating Feng Shui is to begin with one room. Stand in the doorway of the room, with your back to the door, looking into the room. For the purposes of this exercise, assume that your door is north and that you are facing south. Imagine the room laid out in nine squares, three rows of three.

From your position at the entrance to the room, the base-

SOUTHEAST		SOUTH	SOUTHWEST	
	Wealth and Prosperity Wood	Fame and Reputation Fire	Love and Marriage Earth	
EAST	Health and Family Wood	Center	Creativity and Children Metal	WEST
	Wisdom and Knowledge Earth	Career Water	Helpful People and Mentors Metal	
		ENTRANCE		
NORTHEAST		NORTH	NORTHWEST	

Feng Shui ↭ 117

line of the room would be the Wisdom and Knowledge area, the Career area, and the Helpful People and Mentors area. From this spot, you can see how the room is divided and whether there are any missing areas. For example, if you have an odd-shaped room, one of more of the sections might be missing.

Each section has an element and a color assigned to it.

Front Left *Wisdom and Knowledge*

ELEMENT Earth

COLORS Black, blues, and greens

This area of the room represents wisdom, learning, educational pursuits, study. This is where the bookcase goes, if you have only one. . . . Pictures of mentors can be displayed. Anything that you have learned from or expanded your knowledge with should go here. It's a good place for knick-knacks you have learned something about or that have a story behind them. This is the spot for meditation. You may want to make it your reading corner.

Front Middle *Career*

ELEMENT Water

COLORS Black, blue, brown

This area keeps you focused on your career goals. Put your affirmations of things you hope to accomplish under a pyramid or other stone in your career corner. If you are applying for university, include a picture of the university there or a copy of your application or résumé. If you have a picture of someone who is doing what you hope to do in your career, display that picture here.

Front Right Helpful People and Mentors

> ELEMENT Metal
>
> COLORS White, gray, and black

This area represents people unrelated to you who can help you. They can be priests, rabbis, teachers, or anyone else who touches your life and relays knowledge and help to you. This is where the phone should go! Also, phone books and business cards. Some people put angels in this area, signifying help from the dearly departed. Gifts from and photographs of people who have helped and influenced you in any way or books and articles about them should go here.

Middle Left Health and Family

> ELEMENT Wood
>
> COLORS Blues and greens

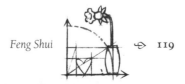

This area represents family, friends, coworkers, distant relatives, physical and emotional health. This is the part of the house you should hang all those happy family memory pictures, to ensure good health for the future. You could put your weights or other workout equipment here, as well as a bowl of fruit or your exercise tapes!

Center

ELEMENT Earth

COLORS Yellow, earth tones

This represents the culmination of all the areas put together, signifying health and longevity.

Middle Right *Creativity and Children*

ELEMENT Metal

COLORS White and pastels

Children and creativity are symbolized by this area. It also affects the development of current projects and any creative endeavors. This area concerns projects you are working on now and your plans for the future. Put articles, photographs, notes relating to current projects in this area. Photographs of children, especially children who are related to you, are especially powerful here. If you are an artist, this is the perfect place to hang your paintings. You could put your piano here or your sewing machine. Anything that signifies creativity in your life.

Far Left *Wealth and Prosperity*

ELEMENT Wood

COLORS Blues, purples, and reds

The southeast corner of a room or building is the wealth or money corner. It signifies money, prosperity, and abundance. Keep it clean and activated. Examine this corner in each of your rooms, and then consider this corner of your house as a whole.

What is in that corner? What can you do to activate more positive energy there? Plants, crystals, aquariums, or lights can activate positive energy flow. Hanging a crystal sun catcher in a window keeps the energy flowing.

Are there cobwebs in that corner? Dust? Photos of people, like an overbearing relative, who make you uncomfortable?

Is there a toilet in that corner? Keep the lid down. Drains of any kind in the money corner can suck your money away.

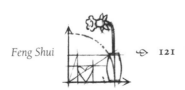

Are you missing that corner because your room is an odd shape? Try to recreate a corner by putting in plants and gemstones, a crystal ball, some chimes, or a mirror.

Is there a fireplace in that corner? That may be why you are having financial concerns. Your money is going up in smoke. Try to counteract that by putting pieces of quartz crystal and citrine along the mantelpiece.

You could light a green or gold candle in that corner during the new moon to activate auspicious energy. Place a pyramid there, with your financial goals written on a piece of paper placed underneath it. Put pieces of citrine or malachite in that corner, even in a potted plant, to ensure growth.

Far Middle *Fame and Reputation*

ELEMENT Fire

COLORS Reds

This area activates energy in how others see you. If fame is important to you, put all records of your achievements in this area. This includes awards, diplomas, certificates, letters of praise, trophies, newspaper clippings. You don't have to display them; you can hide them if you feel shy. This, as well as perseverance, will activate vibrations of even more success.

Far Right Love and Marriage

ELEMENT Earth

COLORS Reds, pinks, and white

The southwest is your love corner. Marriage, partnerships, and love are represented here. Really look at what you have in this corner. Are there dirty clothes, distressing photographs, a filing cabinet? Move the clutter out, or you will have clutter in your love life. Make sure the corner is clear from cobwebs and dust.

Activate positive love vibrations in your life by placing a piece of rose quartz there. Is this a light area of the house or a dark area? Hang a faceted crystal from the ceiling or in the window so that its sparkling flashes will activate auspicious energy.

Is there a toilet or a drain of any kind in that corner? Keep them covered and shut. Fireplaces as well can drain away good energy flow.

Light a red or pink candle on the new moon or on a Friday to stimulate vibrations of love into your life. Tie a red ribbon around a plant pot. Put a pyramid or heart-shaped stone in that corner.

Remember, you can't ask for someone in particular to love you, because this would take away that person's free

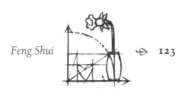

will. But you can ask the universe to open up your heart and mind to any and all possibilities of love coming into your life.

This goes to show that your will can often overcome environmental influences if you believe in yourself and trust the universe.

✧ THE ROOMS OF THE HOUSE

The Entryway

When you first walk through your front door, what do you see? Can you even get in your front door? In good Feng Shui, your front door entrance is free from clutter. The first look into a home from the front door is inviting. Shoes and coats should not block the way into your home. You shouldn't be distracted by clutter or piles of books. You'll want guests and positive energy and spirits to feel comfortable entering your home.

The main entryway of your house, no matter what the size, should be a space unto itself. You might want to get a screen or partition to create the illusion of a hallway if your home opens up to a large, wide space when you first walk in.

Some people put a little fountain just inside the door, within sight of the entrance to the house. Be careful exactly where you put such a fountain. Do not put it on the left-hand side of the front door; the energy created may encourage your spouse to engage in infidelity. A black or blue rug at your front door will attract opportunities into your life.

The Bedroom

Stand in the doorway of your bedroom, and really look at the room before you. What is the first thing that you see? A comfortable, inviting bed? How does the room feel? Is it bright and happy or is it dark and gloomy? Does this room feel inviting and relaxing, or is it busy and chaotic? What colors are prominent? Are they soothing, pale colors or bright stimulating colors?

Where does your eye go? To the bed? To a painting? To a mountain of clutter? What are in the corners? Are there piles of dirty laundry and stacks of papers? Is the garbage can empty?

The purpose of a bedroom is to sleep and have romance. You shouldn't work or even watch TV in there. Getting your bedroom organized should help you rest better and enhance your love life!

Put rose quartz in the love corner of your bedroom. You can even put a little table with two red candles and stones there. Light the two red candles every night for a few minutes

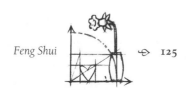

Feng Shui

to attract love into your life or to keep the love that you have vibrant and alive.

When choosing a bed, there are several Feng Shui principles you can keep in mind. Be certain your bed is solid and stable; avoid sleeping on a round bed or a waterbed. Do not use two single beds as a double bed, as this symbolically divides a couple. Bunk beds and canopies are not a good idea; they don't allow the energy to flow freely.

A square headboard is better than a semicircular headboard, since a semicircle suggests that something is missing. Never use a brass headboard. No headboard suggests that the bed is not auspicious.

When positioning your bed, try not to put it under an exposed beam. This symbolically cuts the bed in half, separating a couple. (It also can cause headaches.) Don't put the bed under a window, and never have the bed facing a door or toilet. If possible, the bed shouldn't be located against a wall that has a toilet on the other side. Be certain the bed is raised off the floor, and if possible, don't store anything underneath.

Try to keep the two sides of the bed symmetrical, with matching lamps and night stands. In your master bedroom, be certain that there are no mirrors facing the bed or positioned over the bed, as this can reflect a third party in the relationship of a couple. If there are photographs and paintings in the room, be certain they depict couples and pairs, not solitary figures.

Always keep your bedroom clear of clutter, especially the path from the door to the bed. Be certain there are no plants in the room, as they can drain the room of auspicious vibrations. Plants drain energy—you won't sleep as well. Never put an aquarium behind the bed, because this is bad luck.

If open shelves or sharp edges face the bed, you could get sick. Try not to display sharp pointy objects or paintings, especially above or behind the bed.

It is not a good idea to keep too many books in the bedroom, as this can be too stimulating for rest. Also, keep clocks and phones away from the bed; they provide too much electromagnetic stimulation, which can disturb the sleep cycle. If you keep your clock across the room, you never have to worry about hitting that snooze button!

Try not to put a TV or computer in the bedroom. If because of space concerns you must keep a TV or computer in your bedroom, be certain that it doesn't directly face the bed, as it gives out the same negative energy as a mirror. Cover up the TV when it is not in use, either by keeping it in a cabinet or by draping a scarf across it, and turn it off before you go to sleep.

 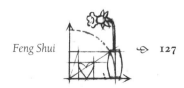

The bedroom is a place of rest and relaxation. It is not a good idea to set up a home office in the bedroom; this will deter you from getting any rest. If you have a small home and you have absolutely no choice but to put your home office in the bedroom, try to block its view from your bed with a screen or partition.

If possible, avoid having exercise equipment in your bedroom. This symbolically suggests that you always have to work on your relationship, or that your relationship is too much work.

Be very careful of master bedrooms with bathrooms located in the southwest corner. Several sources have told me that when this happens, nothing short of moving can be done to stop the negative energy. I happen to have this exact set-up. Coincidence or not, my husband left me a few months after we moved into this home. I didn't know about Feng Shui then and couldn't figure out why for a few years I was not dating or getting on with my love life. When I read about the curse of the master bedroom and bathroom, I realized that was my problem. I couldn't afford to move, nor did I want to, since I enjoy our neighborhood and the children have good friends here. Since there was no way I wasn't going to use that bathroom (as some books suggested), I decided to take my own action. I put lots of gemstones, a couple of rose quartz hearts, and some pyramids in the bathroom. I hung a sun catcher from the shower stall. I try to keep the toilet seat down and the door shut at all times. Things seem to be looking up for me.

Children's and Relatives' Bedrooms

Children, especially sons, should sleep in the east corner of the house. The oldest daughter's bedroom is best located in the southeast corner. Try not to have any dark corners, especially in children's rooms. Be certain to give your children and teenagers privacy: Always knock before entering their rooms. Keep clutter like dirty clothes and candy wrappers at a minimum. Encourage children to put their toys away, out of sight, before they go to sleep, so that they aren't exposed to too much stimulation. Elderly people should sleep in the west corner.

The Bathroom

The bathroom is a very important room in Feng Shui. It is a room of relaxation, and it should not contain a lot of bright and garish colors, although accents are fine. As in the rest of the home, clutter should be kept to a minimum, and all articles that aren't used on a regular basis should be stored or put out of sight. Keep all counter spaces and shelves tidy.

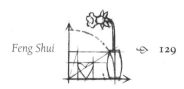

Throw away used and old cosmetics, prescriptions, soaps. Keep the wastebasket empty and the mirror polished.

If possible, try not to locate a bathroom close to the kitchen. If the two rooms must be adjacent, be certain that the bathroom wall doesn't back up to a wall that's used for serving food in the kitchen.

Never install a toilet so that it that faces the front door of the house. If there is a toilet in your southeast corner, it can flush your money away. A toilet in your southwest corner will cause trouble in your marriage. A toilet in the north corner can adversely affect your career. Always keep the toilet seat down when you aren't using it. It's best not to hang a mirror facing the toilet.

Hang mirrors flat against the wall, not jutting out. Magnifying mirrors distort your image and are best avoided. Don't use mirrors that are cut in pieces or tiled. Mirrors of any kind, anywhere in the house, should be hung so that the tallest person in the household doesn't have his or her image cut off.

A dripping faucet is symbolic of wealth dripping away and should be repaired promptly. If a drain gets clogged, unclog it immediately, not only for Feng Shui reasons but for good hygiene as well.

If the bathroom in your master bedroom is in your love corner, be sure to keep all drains covered and the toilet seat down. Putting rose quartz, clear quartz, pyramids, and a prism in my ill-placed bathroom activated vibrations of love, in spite of the doomsaying of the experts. Most of us cannot afford to move in order to accommodate Feng Shui principles, and it isn't terribly practical not to use a convenient bathroom. We have to do the best we can with what we have. I also found that smudging the room now and again helps as well (see chapter 10). It is especially important to keep a bathroom door closed.

The Home Office

Many people have offices in their homes. As mentioned earlier, if it is at all possible, avoid setting up your office in your bedroom. If you must, put up a dividing screen so that you can't see your bed from your office.

If your office ceiling contains an exposed beam, be sure to move your desk as far from the beam as you can. Hang wind chimes on the beam to soften the negative energy. Make sure that your desk chair has a back and arms. Take regular breaks, especially if you are working on a computer.

Try to arrange your office furniture so that you face the door to the office, with your back against a wall. This is the ultimate power position. You are solid against the wall, and no one can sneak up on you.

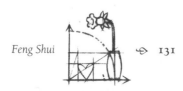

You needn't sit directly in front of the office door; just be sure that you face the door, so that you can see who is coming and going and you are aware of them before they are aware of you. If you are directly in the path of all the energy that flies in the door, you may become overwhelmed. For similar reasons, don't sit at the end of a long corridor. The energy rushing down the hallway at you will be too strong. You can block the energy either with plants or with a door. A cactus plant outside the office door can soften negative energy from hallways, stairs, and outside doors.

I have a U-shaped desk in my office that is positioned in such a way that I can't sit with my back to the wall. To counterbalance the fact that someone could easily sneak up on me while I'm working on my computer, I turn my chair when I am on the phone or reading or making notes so that my back is to the wall. This keeps the energy circulating, and I don't fall into the trap of sitting "exposed."

Avoid sitting with your back to a window. Anyone might be able to sneak up on you on the outside, and unconsciously you will always feel unsettled. Try not to position your desk so that you are looking directly out of a window either, as this is distracting. In my house, I must face out the window when I'm in my office, but I solved my problem by putting up sheer curtains that let in the light but don't allow me to waste time staring out at the world.

If possible, don't sit with your back to an exposed book-case. This can symbolize getting stabbed in the back. It's not good to have water, such as an aquarium or fountain, situated behind you.

Don't sit facing a mirror, which is distracting and causes bad luck. If possible, avoid facing the jutting edges of walls, pillars, or cabinets; the sharp edges will cut into your performance or give you bad luck. If you must face a sharp edge, keep a plant on your desk to soften it. Avoid lights and lamps that have sharp angles and edges.   Always keep your desk tidy, free from clutter. Don't leave leftover food or empty cups on your desk. Keep your garbage can emptied. Keep the desk drawers uncluttered and organized; use filing cabinets, boxes, and storage containers to hold papers and other materials. Discard old, outdated, and unused office supplies. Stay on top of the paper in your In box. Keep a journal that records important information and lists where you can find it instead of leaving loose scraps of paper floating around. Every so often, clear out the clutter from your hard drive.

Put fresh flowers or a small dragon on the left-hand side of your desk. Dragons symbolize good luck. Keep a crystal on

 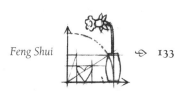

your desk as well. Tie three Chinese coins together with red thread and tape them to the southeast corner of your desk to activate money flow. Or keep them in your checkbook or ledger to attract wealth and good luck. If you are doing world-wide business, keep a globe in your office and spin it daily.

Furniture

How much furniture do you have in your home? Is the space cramped, without room to walk? It's best if there is plenty of room to move freely around your furniture. If the energy can flow freely around your room, this is auspicious energy that will bring more opportunities your way. Is your furniture comfortable? Your guests should feel comfortable, not crowded or cramped.

As with other elements and belongings, it's important that furnishings be in good repair, be used frequently, and be kept clean and free of clutter. If anything is broken or not used very often, repair it or get rid of it. Keep mirrors polished, shelves dusted, and knick-knacks at a minimum.

Fresh flowers brighten up a room and make it feel welcome and inviting. They give off life-affirming positive energy. When flowers begin to droop or die, quickly replace or recycle them. Avoid using dried flowers in your money or love corners.

Always keep extra food on hand. This symbolizes wealth and abundance, activating positive energy to flow your way. To further activate vibrations of wealth, collect loose change and keep it in the far-left corner of your bedroom. Don't leave money lying around.

The Corners of the Room

In each room, be very aware of where the doors, fireplaces, toilets, and windows are, since they can affect energy flow. A room should never have dark corners; you can create energy flow with lights and sunshine. The room should have a sense of balance, both with furnishings and colors.

Sometimes you will see something that looks ominous and you can't do anything about it, such as where the toilet is, or the fireplace, drains, or windows. The best thing to remember is that you want to keep energy moving, not let it get blocked or "sucked away." So, hanging or placing crystals over the offending item is always a good plan. Make sure toilet seats are down, drains are plugged, and doors to those rooms are shut when they aren't in use. You can put a mirror on a bathroom door. Sometimes you can put up a screen to hide the offending item or to create a corner, changing the room shape. You will notice that there seems to be no good place to have a toilet. And you would be right, as far as I can

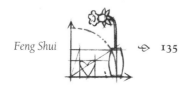

tell. The only thing to do, short of having an outhouse, is keep the lid down and the door shut. Some placements are worse then others, but for the most part, they are all pretty negative and it can feel quite overwhelming. This is where positive thinking and taking things one small step at a time can be important!

⊷ BRINGING IT ALL TOGETHER

Feng Shui

The ancient system of Feng Shui is designed to provide harmony with the environment.

One can use the compass method of Feng Shui, the simpler Pa Kua or Ba Gua method, or a combination of both to create auspicious energy in one's home.

Even performing a few Feng Shui tips will bring good luck into your home.

THE FIVE ELEMENTS

The concept of Feng Shui is built on harmonizing the elements: wood, fire, earth, metal, water.

THE COLORS

When decorating a room, use colors that will encourage the kind of energy you want to draw into your house.

THE NINE SECTIONS

Use the chart to understand what each of the nine sections of your room and house represents.

Activate your love and wealth corners. Energize your other corners with pictures, knick-knacks, candles, and plants.

Don't get overwhelmed by the placement of things you have no control over, such as bathrooms and fireplaces.

THE ROOMS OF THE HOUSE

Pay special attention to your bedroom to ensure romance and good health.

Be aware of where your bathrooms are placed and how they are designed, and what you can do to reverse any negative energy they can bring in. Keep toilet seats down and bathroom doors closed.

Make the most of your home office, to bring wealth and prosperity your way.

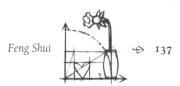

Make sure your furniture is in good repair. Don't have too much furniture in a room. Pay special attention to the corners of each room to be sure energy is flowing into them.

6

AUSPICIOUS SYMBOLS & OBJECTS

Symbols and statues positioned in strategic places around your home can help to accelerate the positive vibrations you are activating by practicing House Magic. Some symbols, such as eggs, may be familar to us. We know that eggs abound at Eastertime and we can intuit that they indicate birth, rebirth, fertility, and springtime. Eggs are also good for creativity. Other symbols, such as turtles and frogs, may be more obscure for North Americans. Shapes, such as round-leafed plants or obelisks, are also meaningful. According to the principles of Feng Shui (see chapter 5), you can place the symbol or object that you select on your altar or in an appropriate position in your home. You can place pyramids, balls, or any number of different items in corners or areas that you want to charge.

Ankh

The ankh is an ancient symbol that represents the key of life. It can be used to enhance creativity, wisdom, and fertility.

Clusters

You've seen them in the stores: natural clusters of stones, sometimes decorated with air plants or little pewter statues. Clusters of citrine will activate vibrations of abundance and creativity. Amethyst will promote healing and release from addictions. There are many types of clusters to choose from, so decide which one is for you. Clusters bring a sense of harmony and balance into the home.

Chinese Coins

You can find Chinese coins in many of the emporiums in your local Chinese district, if you live in an urban area, or you can order them through catalogs. On some Chinese coins, the yang side has four Chinese characters, while the yin has two. These coins are the easiest to use.

Tie three Chinese coins yang side up with red thread or string. There is no specific way to do this, just make sure the yang sides are all on the same side. Three coins tied with red string are an auspicious tool for creating prosperity. Red string activates the essence of good fortune that is symbolized by the coins.

Hang the bundle of coins yang side up on the inside handle of your front door or the main door leading into your house to attract prosperity into your home. On the outside handle of the door, hang a small bell to attract good fortune. Do not hang coins on the back door or on the outside of the door; coins on the outside handle of a door will cause good fortune to slip away!

You can also bury the three coins tied with a red thread under the walkway that leads into your home.

Coins in a red packet can be given as an offering of wealth and luck. This is an excellent gift for friends and family on any occasion, especially for a house warming.

Crystal and Other Balls

Crystal balls are known mostly for *scrying,* or reading the future. You can activate positive energy in your home by having balls made of various stones around the house or in a decorative bowl. A big ball of obsidian, for example, will absorb negative energy. If someone who drains you emotionally is coming to visit, put out a big ball of obsidian. Fluorite balls bring order to chaos; rose quartz activates healing and unconditional love. Regular crystal will absorb negative energy as well as activate psychic vibrations.

Eggs

In many traditions, especially in Alchemy and Metaphysics, the egg is considered a self-contained universe because it represents the five elements prevalent in spiritual disciplines. The outer shell is the earth, the white is water, the membrane connecting to the shell is air, the yolk is fire, and the embryo is spirit.

Eggs symbolize creativity and fertility. Some cultures believe that carrying eggs can help women conceive. Eggs activate ideas, growth, and endless possibilities. They can represent endings and beginnings and rebirth. Eggs have been used for centuries in religious rituals and often provoke philosophical ideas. The white of the egg can represent heaven, while the egg itself represents earth; in other forms of thought, the white of the egg is the moon and the yolk of the egg is the sun. These ancient ideas make the egg a powerful tool.

To activate the power of eggs, stand in the doorway facing into the room being used. To attract love, place an egg in the far right-hand corner of the room. To attract prosperity, place an egg in the far left-hand corner of the office or business.

Fish

If you have live fish, it's good to have nine of them. One should be black to absorb negative energy; the rest should be orange or red to activate good fortune and prosperity. It is thought that if a fish dies, it has absorbed negative energy. You needn't worry about that; just get a new one so that you always keep the number at nine.

To activate prosperity, keep an aquarium of goldfish (one

black) in the southeast corner of your living room. Living plants and other natural elements should be in the tank as well. Angular fish like angelfish can create negative vibrations that could cause you to lose money, so it's best to avoid them. Keep the tank clean or you will clog your good fortune with negative energy.

Fish-shaped objects also bring positive energy into the home. A crystal fish on a northwest table is a good luck symbol. Put a double fish symbol that is gold or a drawing under the mattress where your head rests. This will provide you with protection and will attract good opportunities.

Frogs

The three-legged frog with a coin in his mouth is an excellent symbol to use inside your home. You can find one in your city's local Chinatown if you live in an urban area. They come in various sizes and can be made of wood or stone.

The frog draws in vibrations of prosperity, so it is important that he is looking into your home, not out the door. If he is looking out a door or window, your money might leave you. He should be near the front door, but not on the floor. He can be placed on a low table in your living room. For wealth and career luck, place the frog in the northwest corner of the room or house.

Medicine Bags and Pouches

You can buy a little pouch or make one to create your own medicine bag. You can have several that you wear at different times for different reasons, or just one that you carry with you at all times. You may hang it from your neck or waist, or you may conceal it. It is your personal choice.

Using the information in this book, you can create your own pouch and fill it with gemstones, herbs, or a wish written on a piece of parchment and tied up with a string of the color of the energy you hope to attract. For example, if you are hoping to attract vibrations of prosperity you might want to put the following items in your pouch:

CITRINE for creative growth and prosperity

MALACHITE for good luck and prosperity

QUARTZ CRYSTAL to absorb negative energy

TIGER EYE for courage and the strength to achieve goals

APACHE TEARS for protection against harm

A tiny piece of PARCHMENT with a wish written on it, then rolled into a scroll and tied with green and gold thread

Other items you might want to put in a medicine bag are sage, sweetgrass, tobacco, or cedar. (See chapter 10.)

Obelisks

An obelisk has four sides and a top like a pyramid. It is good for activating energy. According to Feng Shui, you can write a wish on piece of parchment paper and put it underneath the obelisk on your altar or in the section of the room you want to activate energy.

Octahedrons

Octahedrons are often used to bring order to chaos. They are good for analyzing and for healing. I carry a purple fluorite one in my pocket if I am having cramps.

Pillows

You can make a little pillow with special herbs and stones to help you sleep better or to help you remember your dreams. You can place a piece of citrine in it to dispel nightmares. Some herbs, like valerian, will give you vivid dreams, while chamomile will relax you. A pillow can be tied onto the back of a favorite chair or placed under a couch cushion.

You can keep little pillows in the car to calm the kids during long car rides.

Prisms

Prisms create a rainbow of colors dancing around the room. This can generate positive vibrations, especially for someone who may be missing a color or is feeling depleted of energy. Prisms are good for deflecting "poison arrows" or bad luck, especially if you have a bed or a desk in an inauspicious place and are unable to move it.

Pyramids

As we all know, the pyramid is a powerful tool. It works by focusing and amplifying energy.

For wish fulfillment, write down your wish on a piece of paper and keep it under your pyramid for seven days. Visualize your wish coming true. On the seventh day, burn your paper.

To activate prosperity, place a bill of any denomination under the pyramid in the money corner of your house or bedroom or altar, which is the far-left corner from the doorway as you enter a room. Visualize your life filling with wealth and happiness.

If you want a new car or any other new possession, place a picture of it underneath the pyramid.

Remember, the spirit energy will send to you what you need to experience. Be prepared to accept your fate!

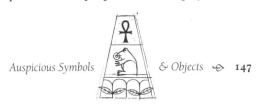

Turtles and Tortoises

The turtle symbolizes good fortune, protection, and longevity; it also attracts the assistance of helpful people.

Place a turtle in the east corner of the room for good health. Place a turtle in the north for wealth. The turtle can be alive or a statue. Since turtles are solitary creatures, you only need one.

Wands

Wands have been used for centuries to conduct energy for magical and health purposes.

Cleanse your wand when you first receive it by washing it in spring water with a pinch of sea salt. Be sure to cleanse it before each ritual you perform with it. Let it dry in the light of the sun and moon on your altar or windowsill.

Welcome your wand into your life by burning sage or incense and holding it in the smoke. You may decorate it with copper, gemstones, feathers, leather, or anything else that has meaning for you. Or you may choose to leave it plain.

Treat your wand with respect, and never point it at anyone in jest.

Auspicious Symbols & Objects

There are many symbols of good luck and prosperity—such as citrine clusters, coins, and fish—that you can place around your home to activate positive energy.

To be sure you are activating the energy you wish for, always double-check the placement and direction of the objects you use.

7

PLANTS, FOUNTIANS & MIRRORS

Plants, tabletop fountains, and mirrors not only brighten a home, but they are great for activating auspicious vibrations. In and of themselves, they are all excellent generators of auspicious energy. Keep in mind, though, that the placement of any of these items is crucial. In the wrong spots, these same items can create negative energy.

☙ PLANTS

Plants symbolize growth and creativity. (You'll remember that in chapter 4, on astrology, we listed the plants that relate to each sun sign.) They work particularly well in the corners of a room to keep the air flowing instead of stopping dead. The Chinese jade plant is the most auspicious of the plants. If you can't find a jade plant, you can also use a little tree made out of jade stones for the same purpose.

Plants that stand upright and have pointed leaves are good for moving energy and should be placed in the south part of the home and in corners. Plants that have round leaves and that droop are good for the north side of the home, as they provide calming energy. If you have exposed overhead beams, creeper plants will soften the corners.

According to the principles of Feng Shui (see chapter 5), plants can shield and dissolve "poison arrows"—negative energy, espionage, liars, backstabbers, bad luck, money loss, or anything else that doesn't work in our favor. To counteract poison arrows, put a plant in front of a protruding edge, especially on a corner that juts out. You may place a pair of large cactus outside of the door of an office to deflect negative energy from main doors and elevators.

Plants in the southeast corner activate vibrations of wealth, so it is excellent to put plants in the wealth corner of your room or house. Any healthy plants with broad leaves will activate wealth. It is never a good idea to have dried, dying plants or driftwood in the wealth corner or the love corner of your home.

Plants can keep you from sleeping, so it is best not to put them in the bedroom. They will drain your energy.

Wherever you have plants or flowers in the house, always keep them looking fresh. Remove dead, dying, or sickly looking leaves and flowers. Silk flowers—but not plastic ones— are just as good as real ones. Silk maple and ficus trees are great to have. Remember to replace artificial plants once a year, or whenever they begin to fade. Pictures and paintings of flowers and wooden replicas of flowers are good too.

Nothing is quite as pleasurable as a tabletop fountain. These are becoming increasingly popular as decorative items. It is always good luck to have water moving in the home, whether it is from a fountain or an aquarium.

A small perpetual water fountain attracts good luck and wealth. The best place to put it is on the north side of the living room. Be certain not to use a fountain so large that it overwhelms the room, as this will drown the good luck energy you are trying to activate.

Water of any kind (fountain, aquarium, toilet) should not be located under a staircase, especially if there are children in the house, as it can create bad energy and may in particular cause problems with school, learning, and bad luck.

Fountains and aquariums are not good for the bedroom. If you place an aquarium behind a bed, you may be robbed or cheated.

❧ **MIRRORS**

Mirrors can be used for scrying, much like crystal balls, and we can see into the future and see who we were in the past by looking into mirrors. Mirrors represent reflection: reflection as in remembering, reflection as in seeing the truth, reflection as in considering possibilities. Mirrors in a dream are often symbols of self-examination. If you dream about mirrors, it is time to examine who you are, what you want, who you want to be. It is time to clean up your act; we can all do that no matter how clean we think our acts are! The mirror can represent hundreds of other things too, from narcissism to a gateway, as in *Alice through the Looking Glass*.

Mirrors can create auspicious energy, but again, consider their placement with great care. Mirrors can both attract and repel energy. If you have moved any mirrors and find that your luck is getting worse instead of better, reconsider the new placement of the mirror.

An auspicious place for a mirror is in the dining room. The bigger the mirror, the better. It reflects the food being eaten, symbolically doubling the prosperity in the home.

If you are missing a corner in your home, or have an empty space, you can put a mirror there to activate positive energy flow. However, you must be certain that the mirror doesn't reflect the front door, a toilet, or a staircase. Mirrors can activate positive energy flow when used in dark corners or in long hallways.

Be certain that all mirrors are hung so that the tallest person in the house doesn't have the image of her head cut off.

For this reason, the use of tiled mirrors is frowned upon; the tiling represents the cutting up of the image.

Try not to place mirrors opposite the front door, opposite the bed, opposite windows, or opposite each other. If a mirror reflects the front door or any windows, any good luck being drawn in will immediately be reflected back outside again.

A mirror in the bedroom shouldn't face the bed. This goes for dresser mirrors, small cabinet mirrors, ceiling mirrors, televisions, and so on. Mirrors facing a bed can cause havoc in marriage. They creates misunderstandings and sometimes reflect a third party. If a mirror does face the bed, keep the mirror covered with a colorful scarf or other piece of material. The same goes for the television set when you aren't using it.

Mirrors facing each other create restless energy.

Try not to sit with a mirror facing you, especially in your office.

Pa Kua Mirrors

A Pa Kua mirror is a circle mirror in wood surrounded by eight trigrams. This mirror has three lines at the top, which usually has a little hook from which to hang it, but if the hook is missing, it should be hung so that the trigram with three unbroken lines is on the top. Be certain the mirror isn't upside down.

A Pa Kua mirror should never be used inside the home. It can be used outside of the home to deflect bad energy or poison arrows, but try not to deflect them back to your neighbors. You'll want to be certain that the way you position the mirror doesn't inadvertently cause bad luck for your neighbors.

Because the Pa Kua mirror is so powerful, you might want to read more about Feng Shui and the use of Pa Kua mirrors before you use one. Useful sources on Feng Shui are listed in the References.

↭ BRINGING IT ALL TOGETHER

Plants, Fountains & Mirrors

PLANTS

Plants can activate creative growth and financial success.

Choose and place your plants wisely, to attract positive energy. Keep energy flowing in your corners by placing a plant.

Don't put dried flowers or potpourri in your romance or money corners! Keep plants and flowers watered and fresh looking. Discard dying or dead plants.

FOUNTAINS

Fountains are beautiful ways to keep the energy flowing through your environment.

Watch your placement of an indoor fountain; try to find the most auspicious place for it.

MIRRORS

Mirrors can both attract and repel energy.

Be careful where you place your mirrors. Your good luck can bounce right outside if a mirror reflects your front door. Try not to place mirrors opposite the bed, opposite windows, or opposite each other.

Take great care when hanging a powerful Pa Kua mirror outside your home.

8

CRYSTALS
& GEMSTONES

Precious gifts from the Earth can activate positive vibrations, especially when they're placed in auspicious areas around the home. It's great to put a gemstones under your pillow, or you can create a "dream" pillow, which is a little pillow filled with herbs and stones to help you sleep. You can carry gemstones in your wallet or purse; you can put them in your pocket or bra; you can make a little pouch to wear around your neck or hang from your rearview mirror in the car. You can sew stones into your clothes, tape them under your desk, or stash them in your glove compartment. You can put them on your altar, in your fountain, on your mantle. Anywhere that they will bring auspicious energy, such as rose quartz in your family corner, is appropriate.

✦ CHOOSING A STONE

You've decided you want a gemstone or crystal for yourself. But how do you go about selecting one?

Sometimes we receive stones as gifts. But usually we decide we need a particular stone, so off we go to seek one out. The obvious places to look for stones would be New Age shops, occult stores, online sites, and fantasy conventions. Be careful that you don't end up paying a huge price for what is essentially a hunk of rock. Of course, tumbled stones cost more than rough stones, and faceted stones, especially those set in jewelry (like diamonds), can run into the thousands of dollars. It doesn't matter how "rough" your stone is—the end result will be the same.

Some of the more economical places to get stones are mineral stores that sell stones in bulk, rock and mineral conventions, and little stores that specialize in Mexican or South American wares and beads. If you have a business, you can try to get your stones wholesale at a beading company or similar place.

How do you know which one to choose? There are lots of ways to tell. The most simple and obvious one is that a stone catches your eye. So buy it! Many times I'll go searching for one type of stone and end up with several other types. Sometimes stones just seem to want to go home with me.

You can rub your hands together, as you learned in chapter 1, to get the energy flow started, and then hold your hands over various stones. Some will feel stronger or better than others. Go with the ones that feel good to you.

Pick up a stone. Hold one in your hand. You can hold it with your thumb and first finger or close it in your palm. Feel the stone's vibrations. Are they strong or weak? Do they make you feel good, or are they too much for you?

Some people like to find stones in the earth. That's fine too.

Sometimes stones just come mysteriously into our lives. And sometimes they go out of our lives, by getting lost, or because they have been given away to someone who admires them. That's okay. It is all part of the cycle of life. If a stone disappears, it wasn't meant to be with you at that time. So just move on.

Don't worry if the stone that feels right to you isn't the prettiest. Surface markings, scuffs, chips, and inclusions will have no affect on the stone's properties.

⚘ CLEANSING A STONE

Stones should be cleansed when you first get them to clear out the vibrations of those persons who have handled them before you. Also, some people like to clear their stones periodically, especially if it seems like their potency has "worn" out or if someone they don't like has touched them.

There are many ways to cleanse a new stone. You can leave it on the windowsill, so the rays of the new moon or the full moon can bathe it. You can hold it over a burning sage stick or incense. You can bury it in the earth in the full moon and dig it up on the new moon. You can put it on a slab of marble or some other cleansing rock. You can soak it in a mixture of sea salt and spring water for a few hours or days. (Some stones have soft surfaces and don't respond well to soaking with sea salt, so if in doubt, ask about the best cleansing method when you buy the stone.)

When you have finished cleansing your stone, you should carry it with you for a few days. You should carry your stone around so that it gets to "know" you, or in other words, your energy goes into it. Also, the energy of the stone can work for you while you carry it, and some people always carry stones on them somewhere, in their pockets, bras, or little satchels they hang around their necks.

⟜ PROGRAMMING A STONE

Once your stone is cleansed, you have to give it instructions on why it is here in your life. You can do this by performing a spell or affirmation. You can simply hold the stone in your hand between your thumb and first finger and tell it what you want it to do.

Keep the programmed stone close to you for a few days.

↭ STONES AND SUN SIGNS

Different stones vibrate to different astrological signs. That means that to achieve the stone's optimum effect, it's related sign should be considered when choosing the stone. For example, a Gemini might carry a piece of howlite to help deal with stress, or an Aquarius might carry a garnet for protection.

↭ STONES AND NUMBERS

Similarly, different stones vibrate to different numbers. This all has to do with energy. Gemini is ruled by the twins, so the number 2 fits right in. The number 2 might be in your birth name or fate number, if you do numerology. Maybe your house number contains a 2. There are all sorts of ways to read the numbers.

Each letter of the alphabet is associated with a number, as represented by the following chart.

1	2	3	4	5	6	7	8	9
A	B	C	D	E	F	G	H	I
J	K	L	M	N	O	P	Q	R
S	T	U	V	W	X	Y	Z	

You can use this grid to find the numbers included in your name as well as those numbers that are missing from it, and then, using the information at the end of this chapter, find what stones or crystals vibrate to those numbers. Using crystals and stones with numbers that already exist in your name will help you become aware of the experiences you have had and are having, and help you understand why these things are happening and how to handle them. If numbers are missing from your name or birth date, you might want to add to your altar or fountain stones that will activate your missing vibrations; such stones represent experiences you are missing and need to have to continue your spiritual journey, including reincarnating to the next level. You can usually find answers if you sit and study and contemplate what the stones with your missing number vibrations are and what they represent.

This is all related to the idea of keeping things in balance and in harmony. The chakras, numbers, stones, and everything else on this planet and in this universe are all whirling vortexes of energy.

To further your understanding about stones and numbers, consider reading *Love Is in the Earth*, a fantastic book. You can also read books on numerology. The *Numerology Workbook* by Julia Line and *Chinese Numerology* by Richard Webster are good, straightforward books that will help you understand numbers and what they mean.

I have tried to list here stones and crystals that can be easily found.

AMBER Ruled by Leo and Aquarius
Vibrates to the number 3

Amber is a calming stone that can transform negative energy into positive energy. This is a good stone for purifying a room, creating balance and order.

AGATE Ruled by Gemini
Vibrates to the number 7

There are a multitude of types of agate, each with a particular quality and vibration. Agate balances the yin-yang energy, creating harmony in one's self by transforming and eliminating negative energy.

AMAZONITE Ruled by Virgo
Vibrates to the number 5

Amazonite activates the heart chakra, giving you the will and energy to communicate with loved ones. It is a calming, soothing stone that balances the yin-yang energies and dispels negative influences.

AMETHYST Ruled by Pisces, Virgo, Aquarius, Capricorn
Vibrates to the number 3

This popular crystal is often used for meditation, especially when problem solving. It is reputed to help get rid of headaches and other health concerns. Amethyst can absorb negative energy and provide a state of harmony in a room.

APACHE'S TEAR Ruled by Aries
Vibrates to the number 6

Apache's tear is created from volcanic glass and is a type of obsidian. It is used for comfort in times of grief. It can provide insight in times of distress and can encourage forgiveness. Carry it with you for good luck and protection.

AQUAMARINE Ruled by Gemini, Pisces, Aries
Vibrates to number 1

Aquamarine activates psychic powers. It brings joy, peace, and happiness. It helps you to be more aware of situations and can activate positive energy flow in relationships. Carry it with you while traveling to keep storms from ruining your trip.

AVENTURINE Ruled by Aries
Vibrates to the number 3

Aventurine activates vibrations of creativity and good luck. It is considered by many to be a money magnet. This stone helps heal and soothe both emotional and physical problems.

BERYL (GOLDEN) Ruled by Leo
Vibrates to the number 1

Beryl can protect you from psychic vampires—people who drain your energy—and manipulators. If you have misplaced something, holding beryl can help you "see" where it is by activating your memory and intuitive sense. Beryl can provide motivation at times when you're just not in the mood to do anything.

BLOODSTONE Ruled by Aries, Pisces, Libra
Vibrates to the numbers 4 and 6

Bloodstone is useful for healing and combating stress. It can activate vibrations of courage and creativity. It's also useful for acts of renewal in friendship, love, and other relationships. It can be worn to promote physical strength.

CARNELIAN Ruled by Taurus, Cancer, Leo
Vibrates to the number 5 and 6

Carnelian provides courage for those involved in public speaking or performance, including actors and musicians. It can activate vibrations of love, especially among family members, and promote stability. It can inspire creativity, compassion, and energy. Carnelian can reduce feelings of envy, doubt, rage, apathy, and sadness. It provides protection against nightmares and psychic vampires.

CAT'S EYE Ruled by Capricorn, Taurus, Aries
Vibrates to the number 6

Cat's eye can provide protection and in ancient times was thought to render people invisible. It can be used to guard wealth and to help with financial decisions.

CHRYSOTILE Ruled by Taurus
Vibrates to the numbers 8 and 55

Chrysotile is a good stone to have for achieving goals and wishes. The energy can also help to release baggage from the past. It activates vibrations of integrity, honesty, and re-sourcefulness.

CITRINE Ruled by Gemini, Aries, Libra, Leo
Vibrates to the number 6

Everyone should carry a piece of citrine in her wallet to activate vibrations of prosperity. This crystal can be used to enhance creativity, absorb negative energy, and cleanse the aura. It is great for enhancing business or school and for working through family challenges. Putting a piece of citrine under your pillow is said to help dispel nightmares, or at least help you to analyze them better.

COPPER Ruled by Taurus and Sagittarius
Vibrates to the number 1

Copper is good for bringing good luck and finding lost objects. It activates optimism, initiative, and independence. It can bring philosophical thought without judgment and is useful in psychic work.

DIAMOND Ruled by Leo, Aries, Taurus
Vibrates to the number 33

Diamond can be used for strength, self-confidence, and courage. Contrary to popular belief, it is not a symbol of love but of fidelity. It can be useful in combating sexual dysfunction. Diamond can bring peace and reconciliation.

EMERALD Ruled by Taurus, Gemini, Aries
Vibrates to the number 4

Emerald can activate energy to bring domestic bliss and loyalty. It is also good for psychic work, focus, and intensity. It can be useful in bringing about a successful conclusion to legal work.

FLUORITE Ruled by Pisces and Capricorn
Different types vibrate to different numbers

Fluorite is one of my favorite stones, not only for its beautiful vibrant purples and greens, but because it brings order to chaos! It can help increase concentration and restore balance by allowing you to see the truth in a situation. Fluorite is also valuable for bringing together groups or families by providing a stabilizing energy.

GARNET Ruled by Leo, Virgo, Capricorn, Aquarius
Vibrates to the number 2

Garnet represents commitment, devotion, and understanding. It is also useful for strength, endurance, and protection.

HEMATITE Ruled by Aries and Aquarius
Vibrates to the number 9

Hematite is good for grounding, especially if you are spaced out after meditating. It brings a calming atmosphere, dissolves

negative energy, and restores balance. Putting it on your forehead can calm a fever by drawing the heat into the coolness of the stone. It helps the brain process technical and mathematical information.

HERKIMER DIAMOND Ruled by Sagittarius
Vibrates to the number 3

This stone can be used to provide harmony and balance. It stimulates clairvoyant and clairaudient abilities as well as telepathic abilities.

HOWLITE Ruled by Gemini
Vibrates to the number 2

Howlite's presence can soothe pain, anger, and stress. It can also buffer rudeness and obnoxious behavior by activating vibrations of subtlety and tact.

JADE Ruled by Aries, Gemini, Taurus, Libra
Vibrates to the number 11

Jade can help with dream recall. It provides self-confidence, self-reliance, and self-sufficiency. Jade assists with wisdom and the ability to anticipate the needs of others. It brings loyalty and fidelity in relationships.

JET Ruled by Capricorn
Vibrates to the number 8

Jet can provide protection against illness and violence. It is also a good stone to have for business and helps to stabilize finances. Its calming energy helps with depression.

LAPIS LAZULI Ruled by Sagittarius
Vibrates to the number 3

Lapis lazuli is a great stone for psychic work, as it helps to bring together total awareness. It can protect from physical danger and psychic attacks. A good stone for depression, it activates vibrations of serenity and self-acceptance. It also brings success to relationships.

MALACHITE Ruled by Capricorn, Scorpio
Vibrates to the number 9

Malachite is one of my favorite stones because of its beautiful green color and interesting swirls. You can keep this stone in a cash register or wallet to attract prosperity. It is also a great healing stone and provides protection, especially in traveling. It provides insight, balance, fidelity, and loyalty.

MOLDAVITE Ruled by Scorpio
Vibrates to the numbers 2 and 6

Moldavite is a tektite, a piece of meteor or moon or planet that falls to earth. It resembles glass. Many people believe that it is a way to communicate with extraterrestrial beings. It is a good stone for psychic work and dream awareness. Rubbing it on your hands enables you to pick up vibrations better when you are reading people.

MOONSTONE Ruled by Cancer, Libra, Scorpio
Vibrates to the number 4

Moonstone reflects Nature's cycles, enabling us to be more aware of new beginnings. Good for introspection, intuition, and insight, it helps you make decisions that will further your development.

OBSIDIAN Ruled by Sagittarius
Vibrates to the number 1

Obsidian absorbs negative energy. A ball of obsidian in the living room or office can help to stabilize the effect of people who create stress. It provides protection against people and events that can cause you harm.

ONYX Ruled by Leo
Vibrates to the number 6

Onyx is useful in situations where you need self-control. It helps when dealing with grief. This stone brings vibrations of happiness and good fortune.

OPAL Ruled by Cancer, Libra, Pisces, Scorpio
Vibrates to the number 8

Opal brings faithfulness and loyalty to loved ones, friends, and business partners. Heightening the senses, this gemstone is good for psychic and mysticism work. It is great for memory retention, and also good for dreams and wish fulfillment.

PEARL Ruled by Cancer and Gemini
Vibrates to the number 7

Pearl can provide a calming influence and is good for psychic work. It can help you to see the truth in the situation. It brings faith and focus into your life.

PERIDOT Ruled by Virgo, Leo, Scorpio, Sagittarius
Vibrates to the numbers 5, 6, and 7

Peridot helps to calm anger and jealousy. It provides protection against outside influences such as job stress, world events, and societal aggravations. It can help you to recognize the changes in your life.

QUARTZ Ruled by all astrology signs
Vibrates to the number 4

Quartz is a popular stone that comes in many types that activate various vibrations. Clear quartz is the most popular form for wands and crystal balls. Wearing a quartz crystal necklace will help you to think more clearly and will activate psychic energy. It is very useful for meditation and esoteric work of all kinds.

ROSE QUARTZ Ruled by Taurus and Libra
Vibrates to the number 7

Rose quartz activates vibrations of the giving and receiving of universal unconditional love. It can heal heartache and soothe disappointment. It also teaches us how to be accepting of and love ourselves. You can put a piece in the love corner of your bedroom or living room to attract love into your life. Carrying one in your bra or pocket has proven effective in attracting prospective lovers.

RUBY Ruled by Leo, Scorpio, Cancer, Sagittarius
Vibrates to the number 3

Ruby will help you to stabilize your finances. It can help to repel nightmares and unhappiness. It is good for lucid dreaming. It provides creativity and can promote awareness.

SAPPHIRE Ruled by Virgo, Libra, Sagittarius
Vibrates to the number 2

Sapphire brings joy to all who wear it, as well as enhancing intuition. It can activate desires that have been buried in the unconscious to surge forth and manifest wish fulfillment and desires. Sapphire helps achieve focus and rids the mind of intrusive thoughts.

SODALITE Ruled by Sagittarius
Vibrates to the number 4

Sodalite is good for activating self-esteem and self-awareness. It is used for recognizing the truth in your emotions. This stone will enable you to trust yourself and trust others.

TIGER EYE Ruled by Capricorn
Vibrates to the number 4

Tiger eye is good for activating psychic abilities. It enhances perception by bringing balance to the brain. It can activate wealth and the stability to maintain it.

TURQUOISE Ruled by Sagittarius, Pisces, Scorpio
Vibrates to the number 1

Turquoise is good for grounding and promotes inner peace. It provides protection. Some say that it will turn colors to warn of danger or infidelity. It enhances trust, wisdom, and understanding. It can initiate love.

TOURMALINE Ruled by Libra
Vibrates to the number 2

Tourmaline is good for inspiration and self-confidence. It has been used throughout history as a stone for insight into problems. It is used for healing and protection.

Crystals & Gemstones

Gemstones can provide us with energy to manifest what we desire. You can use stones by themselves, keep them on your altar, wear them in your clothes, or carry them in a pouch.

CHOOSING A STONE

Find the stone that is perfect for you by using your eyes, hands, and intuition.

CLEANSING A STONE

Cleanse your stone, using any of several methods, to clear out old energies.

Program your stone by telling it, through spells, rituals, or affirmations, what you want it to do for you. Keep the stone close to you so that it will activate the necessary vibrations into your life.

STONE AND SUN SIGNS

Each kind of stone is ruled by one or several astrological sun signs. Being aware of a stone's relationship to its sign helps ensure that the stone is used most powerfully.

STONES AND NUMBERS

Each kind of stone vibrates to one or more numbers. You can find the number of your birth name, or any numbers that are missing from it, and select a stone that will work most auspiciously for you.

TYPES OF POPULAR STONES

There are many, many different kinds of stones or crystals available, each of which has different properties and different powers. For example, amethyst promotes healing, and combats addictions; obsidian absorbs negative energy. Choose the stone that's best for you and what you want to bring into your life!

9

CANDLES

C andles are very important tools for creating and focusing energy. Candles help bring together your focus, your words, and the vibrations of color and intent. The color of the candle you use is important if you are trying to do something specific, such as bring love into your life. As we all know from science class, color is different vibrations of light energy, and as we've learned in this book, each vibration of energy can be used in a different way. This is why you want to have the maximum combination of color, incense, stones, words, and so on, to create the energy you need to achieve your goal.

Phases of the moon should be considered when planning your candle ritual, too. You can perform candle magic during any of the phases of the moon. A simple rule of thumb is, For anything requiring growth and new beginnings, conduct your ritual in the new moon. For tasks requiring contemplation and puzzle solving, conduct your ritual in the full moon. Silver Ravenwolf has several excellent books, such as *To Ride a Silver Broomstick* and *To Stir a Magick Cauldron*, that describe the proper timing of spells and rituals.

Charging the Candle

Charging your candle is like programming your desire or intent into the candle. To charge your candle, rub scented oil on it. Hold the candle in your hands and visualize what you want it to do. If you wish, you can carve your desire, such as a name or an object or a dollar sign, into the candle. Speak an affirmation or a prayer like the ones found in chapter 12 of this book. Your candle is charged and ready for use.

Using the Candle

Chapter 12 ("Rituals and Affirmations") presents a number of ways you can use candles to generate the energy you need to bring into your life the things you wish for. When your ritual is complete, you can save your candle drippings in your pocket or purse to activate vibrations of romance and good luck. Or you can mix them with herbs and create a dream pillow. Some people like to bury candles back into the earth. If your spell or affirmation involves attracting something into your home, bury the candle remains on your property. If it involves repelling something, then bury it away from your property.

Candles ↢ 183

If possible, use a candlesnuffer to put out a candle. And never leave a candle burning if you aren't there to tend to it.

Be certain to thank the Spirit Motherfather when you are finished with your candle ritual.

Candle Meditation

To practice focusing energy, sit comfortably in front of a lit candle. You can sit in a chair or cross-legged on the floor. Be positive you are not sitting in any drafts, so that you can see the results of your work.

Imagine a white light beaming down from the heavens, through your crown chakra, flowing through your body and then into the ground. Feel yourself full of the white light. Concentrate on the flame of the candle in front of you. Imagine the flame growing higher and longer. Keep staring at it until you see it move. Will it to go higher. If you are satisfied that it is you and not a draft willing it go higher, you can will the flame go lower. Manipulate the flame with your eyes. Have it dance from one side to the other. When you are finished, snuff out the candle. Be certain to rest your eyes when you are finished.

Don't be discouraged if you don't get the hang of this right away. It takes many, many sessions for some people to move the flame at all. By moving the candle flame, you are using your energy and your will. You are learning how to direct that energy, and this will help you to conduct energy when working with other systems.

You can increase the strength of your spell by using the appropriate candle color for your goal. If you don't have the appropriate color candle for your spell, just go with a white one. White is good for any spell or affirmation. For example, let's say you want romance. You could light a white candle, red candle, and pink candle. The white would be for your spiritual purposes and to indicate the purity of your intent (for the good of all!). The red candle would be for love and lust, and the pink candle would be for romantic love and romance. Using your intent and some incense, you are creating a vibration that should bring love into your life. To make the spell even stronger, you should perform it on a Friday night during a new moon, and program a stone like rose quartz (see chapter 8) that you can carry with you at all times to activate vibrations of love coming into your life. Of course, you will *not* try to bring someone in particular into your life; that is wrong, as we have discussed.

Perhaps you know what you want in a future lover. Maybe you are tired of being with men who are always between jobs. Light a green candle to indicate money and growth. This could be growth of money and growth of the relationship when your energies are combined! Maybe you want someone ambitious. Add an orange candle. You can see how it works. I am a big believer in creating our own spells and desires, for we all see the world differently and desire things differently.

Following is a list of popular candle colors and the energies that are associated with each.

BLACK	Protection, repelling negativity, binding
BLUE	Protection, spiritualism, creativity
BROWN	Friendships
COPPER	Passion, money goals, growth
GREEN	Healing, monetary success, growth, personal goals
GOLD	Wealth, winning, happiness
ORANGE	Business goals, property, ambition, career goals, legal matters, selling
PINK	Romantic love, romance, caring, nurturing

PURPLE   Psychic ability, secrets

RED   Energy, strength, passion, courage, career goals, lust, love

SILVER   Telepathy, clairvoyance, psychometry, intuition, dreams

WHITE   Spirituality, peace, higher self, purity

YELLOW   Learning, memory, breaking mental blocks

The use of candles and colors together bring the energy up to the next level, so that you are closer to achieving your heart's desire. Use color to bring the maximum advantage to your work!

✦ BRINGING IT ALL TOGETHER

Candles

Candles can help you focus and activate positive energy flow.

CANDLE MAGIC

Charge your candle before you use it, to ensure that it will help bring you the kind of energy you want. Practice controlling a candle flame to develop your will and intent.

Candles   ✦   187

COLORS OF CANDLES

Different colors are associated with different kinds of energy. Choose the color of candle that best reflects your desire.

INCENSE,
OILS &
SMUDGING

Incense and oils are widely available now in a variety of stores and catalogs. Often they are labeled with their ingredients and purpose, which takes away a lot of the guesswork for the modern practitioner. By all means, explore the various kinds and find out what works for you.

Some scents can be overwhelming and activate allergies, so be careful. There are many fragrances I cannot use. Some give me headaches, some give me congestion. Some I just can't stand the smell of. Period. So I experiment with different scents and try to find the ones that please me. Don't forget that strength and scent varies from one brand to another, so if one is overwhelming, maybe another one isn't.

Different scents activate different vibrations. They can be used as incense, oil, perfume, bath salts, spices, candles, whatever you want. Many scents can be used for more than one purpose or can bring several different kinds of energy; such scents appear in several of the following lists. As with stones, there is a diversity of opinion on what is useful for what purpose, so I tried to incorporate the most popular of these ideas.

SCENTS AND SUN SIGNS

The four elements of fire, water, air, and earth are represented by different fragrances and herbs. You can use these scents as incense, oils, bath salts, and so on. The scent for your sun sign may be a scent that works best to help you achieve a certain goal, or maybe it's a scent that you prefer over some others, just for your general pleasure. This information might be useful when gift giving!

Fire Signs: Aries, Leo, Sagittarius

>ALLSPICE Money, luck, healing

>CARNATION Protection, strength, healing

>CEDAR Healing, purification, money, protection

>CINNAMON Spirituality, success, healing, psychic powers, lust, love

>CLOVE Protection, love, money

>FENNEL Protection, healing, purification

>FRANKINCENSE Protection, spirituality

>GINGER Love, money, success, power

>GINSENG Love, protection, healing, lust

>NUTMEG Prosperity, love, luck

>ORANGE Love, luck, money

PEPPERMINT Sleep, love, healing

ROSEMARY Love, lust, healing, sleep

TOBACCO Healing, purification

Water Signs: *Cancer, Scorpio, Pisces*

APPLE Love, healing

APRICOT Love

BANANA Prosperity

BELLADONNA Astral projection, visions

BLACKBERRY Healing, money, protection

CHAMOMILE Money, sleep, love

HEATHER Protection, luck

HEMP Healing, love, visions, meditation

LEMON Purification, love

LICORICE Lust, love, fidelity

LILY Happiness

PEACH Love

RASPBERRY Love, protection

STRAWBERRY Love, luck

Air Signs: *Gemini, Libra, Aquarius*

ALMOND Money, prosperity

ANISE Protection, purification

CARAWAY Protection, lust, health

CHICORY Removes obstacles, frugality

CITRON Psychic powers, healing

CLOVER Protection, money, love, success

LAVENDER Happiness, peace, love

LEMONGRASS Lust, psychic powers

LILY OF THE VALLEY Happiness

MAPLE Love, money

MINT Money, lust, healing

PINE Healing, protection, money

SAGE Wisdom, protection, wishes

SENNA Love

Earth Signs *Taurus, Virgo, Capricorn*

ALFALFA Prosperity, money

BUCKWHEAT Money, protection

FERN Protection, luck, health

HONEYSUCKLE Money, psychic powers, protection

HOREHOUND Protection, healing

MAGNOLIA Fidelity

MUGWORT Strength, psychic powers, healing

OLEANDER Love

PATCHOULI Money, lust

PRIMROSE Protection, love

QUINCE Protection, love, happiness

RYE Love, fidelity

SAGEBRUSH Purification

TULIP Prosperity, love, protection

⟿ INCENSE

Incense comes in several forms: sticks, cones, powder, and cubes. Some people prefer to create their own blends by mixing several scents together. These days, there is no shortage of places to buy incense. Incense can be used on your altar, or you can light it in the section of your home where you are trying to activate energy. Incense and oils are used with spells and affirmations to send the vibrations toward what is desired.

CEDAR Purification, healing

CINNAMON Spirituality, healing, cleansing

CLOVE Money, protection, cleansing

GINGER Money, success, power

LILAC Protection, love

ROSE Love, psychic powers, divination

SAGE Purifying and cleansing

ᴥ OILS

You can use scented oils in many ways. I wear a decorative vial around my neck that contains the oil I use in tarot reading.

For the purposes of House Magic, you will want energizing oils that will activate positive vibrations. You can rub oil on stones. Just be sure to realize that some stones might change color or texture because of their porous nature. You can rub the oil on candles before you burn them, which gives a stronger resonance to your intention.

Rubbing a dab of oil on your forehead, ears, chakra points, or wrists before conducting a ritual or divination can open up your senses to more possibilities. A few drops of oil in a bath can be pleasing to the senses. You can buy a clay light bulb ring and put a drop of oil on it to activate energy.

Following are some of the scents available for oils and the energy they activate.

ALLSPICE Vitality

ALMOND Money

CEDAR Courage

CLOVE Love, lust, purification

EUCALYPTUS Healing

GARDENIA Harmony, healing, love, money, peace

JASMINE Love, meditation, purification

LAVENDER Sleep

LEMONGRASS Psychic powers

LILAC Harmony, psychic powers

MAGNOLIA Meditation, peace, spirituality

MINT Money

PATCHOULI Money, protection

PINE Money

ROSE Love, protection

SANDALWOOD Psychic, spirituality, healing

VANILLA Lust, power, vitality

↭ SMUDGING

Smudging or *smoking* is a term used by Native Americans or First Nations for the practice of burning herbs for cleansing, purification, praying, and other forms of ritual. Sage or sweetgrass is often used in smudging rituals. Sage is used as a purifier and for cleansing negative energy. It can come in a stick or loose, and is sometimes combined with other herbs like cedar. Sweetgrass usually comes in a long braid to signify Mother Earth. This is good for protection.

I have adopted the practice myself and periodically smudge my house. This can help to eradicate "bad vibes," especially if there has been a fight or someone you don't much care for entered your space.

I use smudging before I pray. I have adopted a simple ritual: I walk around the entire floor of my home with my

smudge stick, careful that the smoke wafts through all the corners, where energy can get stuck, and in the bathroom. Then I smudge a smaller circle around my altar, where I conduct my rituals. I usually go around the smaller circle three times. Often I'll let the smudge stick burn until it goes out.

When I want to bless or purify stones or clean my tarot cards, I put my smoking stick into a fireproof bowl and hold the object over the thick smoke. You can "clean auras" by passing the smoking stick along someone's body, dispelling negative energy. You can also cleanse yourself by waving the smoke toward you from the bowl and brushing it along your body, your arms, your legs.

If you are in a pinch, you can substitute incense for smudge to cleanse your room and to bless your stones.

Using a Smudge Stick

Light the stick. Let it burn for a few moments. Blow it out gently. Pieces of the stick will fall off, so whenever you are holding it, hold a clay or other fireproof bowl filled with sand or earth under it. Don't inhale the smoke more than you have to, as it may give you a headache or make you nauseous.

Sage and cedar can also be crumbled into a bowl and lit on fire, much the same way as with a smudge stick.

Using Scents

Here are a couple of examples of recipes for using scents in pillows for specific purposes. You can use a dab of oil or incense cones if you can't find the herbs. In addition to the examples given, you can create your own types of pillows and satchels for your own intent.

SLEEPING AND RELAXING

This Native American recipe will ensure a good night's sleep or will calm children on long car rides: Put equal amounts of catnip, rabbit tobacco, mint, and sage into a little bag or pillow.

FOR VIVID AND MEMORABLE DREAMS

Use the same mixture as the sleep pillow and add rosemary leaves, lavender, and mugwort to ensure vivid and memorable dreams.

Incense, Oils & Smudging

Different scents activate different vibrations. Explore which smells work best for you.

INCENSE

Use incense on your altar or in a room to which you want to bring the energy of your intent. It is a must for spells and affirmations.

OILS

Oils can be used on your body, in your bathtub, and rubbed on stones or candles.

SMUDGING

Smudging—the practice of burning herbs as part of a ritual—cleanses a room of negative energy.

11

ALTARS & SACRED SPACES

I t is important to have an altar, a space of your own where you can keep your stones and candles and perform rituals. This space is your power source. It is the place where you focus your energy and desire so that you can manifest auspicious energy into your home. The more you use the altar, the more it will build up energy, and the more energy is built up, the more power you create.

Now, most people don't have the luxury of having a room they can dedicate as an altar, so you'll have to be creative and use what you can. All you need is a little table that is yours alone and that won't be disturbed by others. It can be a standing table, a folding table, a shelf, or even the top of a trunk.

Cover the table with a cloth. The cloth should entirely cover the surface of the table. It can be plain or you can sew or draw symbols on it. The more you do to create your altar and make it yours, the more powerful it will be.

You should keep your altar cloth as clean as possible. If it is messy or stained, you should change it, no matter how attached to it you might be. If you spill candle wax on your altar cloth, you can pick it off or iron it off. Some people put a working cloth over the top of the altar cloth, so that if they spill wax or oil or are carving things out of wood or creating medicine bags, they don't soil the altar cloth.

Before you set up your altar, cleanse the air with a sage stick. You will need a fireproof bowl filled with sand or dirt for your sage or smudge stick. Ask the universe to bless this space as your own and to dissipate any negative energy surrounding it.

Put your stones, incense, incense holder, and candles on your altar. Some people like to have fresh flowers, pictures of dearly departed ones, a religious icon such as the Virgin Mary or Buddha. I keep a couple of fluorite obelisks on my altar to absorb the chaos around me. I love fluorite and feel that it calms down the household.

You can use any kind of candles you want. Tea lights, pillars, and oil all work fine. I tend to have white candles that I use as a standard in all my work, and I supplement them with various colors according to what I am trying to achieve. A small knife is good for carving wish fulfillment into candles.

Remember basic Feng Shui (see chapter 5), and put your prosperity stones in the money corner, your love stones in your love corner. You might want to have a pentagram of some sort on your altar as well.

If you have a crystal pyramid on your altar, write down your hopes and desires, put the piece of paper under the

pyramid, and keep it there. If you want money coming into your life, put a fake $1 million bill under a pyramid in the money corner of your altar.

If you want love to come into your life, keep silk flowers (pansies) in a flower pot tied with a red ribbon in your love corner. I use real earth and have planted a rose quartz crystal in the soil of the pot as well.

You can put anything you want on your altar. However, each item on your altar should have significance to you and you alone. You can use items of sentimental value or totems or a little broom to sweep the air. Whatever feels good to you.

Once your altar has been set up, again cleanse the air with sage. If your altar is positioned so that you can do so, walk in a circle around it with your sage stick. Hold each item in the thick smoke of the sage stick to bless it. As you hold each object, think about that object, what it means to you, why you put it there, what you hope it can do for you.

For House Magic, this altar or sacred space is as personal as you are. Keep the altar uncluttered. Dust it often, especially if you burn a lot of incense. Some people recommend covering your altar when you aren't actively using it. I leave mine uncovered. I like the idea of the stones and energy vibrating into the air at all times.

Altars and Sacred Spaces

Find a space that is your own to serve as your altar. Cover your altar with a clean altar cloth. The altar cloth can be plain or you can decorate it with symbols that have personal meaning.

Cleanse the room with sage before setting up your altar.

Put meaningful items on your altar. Don't clutter it. Cleanse each item with sage before beginning a ritual or other work with the altar.

You can cover your altar when you aren't working on it, or leave it uncovered.

12

RITUALS & AFFIRMATIONS

In this chapter, I offer examples of rituals and affirmations that can be used for a multitude of purposes. It is my opinion that affirmations are most powerful if you create your own specifically for your situation. The main thing to keep in mind about affirmations is that they help you to focus your intent. Intent is the key to all spells and affirmations. If your intent is there, if you believe in what you are saying, if you really want transformation, you can have it.

The timing of your ritual is important. Each of the days in the week has special powers, as each day is influenced by a different planet. Also, each day has a different color associated with it. The planets, colors, and areas of power of the days of the week are also presented in this chapter. To increase the energy you are calling on, perform your ritual on the day of the week that is most auspicious for manifesting your intent, and incorporate the colors of that day into your ritual, using that color for your candles, altar cloth, or clothing.

Human beings don't transform overnight. Be patient with yourself. Focus your energy on positive action. See what you want come to pass. With concentration and discipline, you can activate the vibrations to create all that you desire.

Visualize what you want and take action.

Since the beginning of time, human beings have used rituals to gain control of their lives. The use of ritual helps us to focus on our goals and to activate the vibrations that will place us in the path of good fortune. By voicing our dreams to the universe, we take the first step toward walking down the path we desire. By voicing our goals to others, we set into motion a ricochet of cause and effect that will eventually help us achieve whatever we want and need.

Under no circumstances should you ever try to remove free will from another human being or manipulate her mind or possessions, especially in spells for love or money.

When performing rituals that involve the manifestation of love or wealth, visualize in general terms the energy of love, money, a new car, a new job coming into your life. You will receive what you are meant to receive. Sending thoughts of light and love to all you encounter will bring you positive energy, and soon you will find your life filling with joy and love!

Stay positive. If you are experiencing setbacks, don't fall into a spiral of negative energy. Everyone has setbacks and challenges. Be creative. Keep your goals in mind.

In the act of performing an affirmation, how your wish can be turned into reality should become clear to you. You can't just say, "I want a new car," and expect to see one outside your door the next day. It could happen, but it's not likely. But you will become more aware of the ways that you can set about bringing one into your life.

You can use affirmations in many ways. Any one of the following suggestions will work for you.

✳ Say your affirmation while looking at yourself in the mirror. This is good for invoking self-confidence, courage, and self-love.

✳ Say your affirmation while holding a stone that's related to the energy you want to invoke.

✳ Say your affirmation while charging your candle (see chapter 9) or carving words into your candle.

✳ Say your affirmation while a candle is burning.

✳ Say your affirmation while creating a pillow or pouch.

✳ Say your affirmation while you're going to sleep.

✳ Say your affirmation whenever you think about it.

Following are the planets and colors associated with each of the days of the week, and some of the goals related to each day. Performing your ritual on the day that is associated with your goal increases the energy that you will draw toward you. (This list is derived from *To Ride a Silver Broomstick* by Silver Ravenwood.)

Sunday

> PLANET Sun
>
> COLOR Gold, yellow
>
> GOAL Health, success, career, ambition, goals, money

Monday

> PLANET Moon
>
> COLOR Silver, white
>
> GOAL Psychic work, dreams/astral travel, imagination

Tuesday

> PLANET Mars
>
> COLOR Red

GOAL Passion, partnerships, courage, swift movement, energy

Wednesday

PLANET Mercury, Chiron

COLOR Orange, light blue, gray

GOAL Wisdom, communication, intelligence, memory, education

Thursday

PLANET Jupiter

COLOR Purple, royal blue

GOAL Business/logic, gambling, social concerns, wealth

Friday

PLANET Venus

COLOR Green, pink

GOAL Romantic love, friendships, beauty, soul mates, artistic ability, harmony

Saturday

PLANET Saturn

COLOR Black

GOAL Binding, protection, neutralization, manifestation

⊷ SUGGESTED RITUALS AND AFFIRMATIONS

The suggestions offered with the verses are suggestions only. You can use the affirmations to bless stones, to create medicine pouches and dream pillows, or anything else! You can use the affirmations provided as models for creating your own.

Ambition

Fill a pouch with pieces of tiger eye, carnelian, howlite, and cedar. Carry it under your clothes to give you that extra push you need to reach your goals.

You can bless a single stone such as tiger eye or carnelian and carry it with you, keep it on your desk, put it on your computer. You could put it in your wealth or career corner.

Write down your goal on a piece of parchment, place a piece of tiger eye or other gemstone on it, and keep it on your altar. Remember always to keep your goal in mind.

The new moon is a good time for new beginnings and new mindsets.

> I call upon my Higher Self
> To fill my life with love and good health.
> I will use kindness and discretion
> As I conquer my goals with determination.
> Help me be fair and just and kind
> Leaving criticism and impatience behind.
> Let me be everything I can be.
> This I ask and give thanks for,
> Blessed be.

Anger

This is a good affirmation to do in the bathtub. Pour in a few drops of lavender, lilac, rose, or gardenia-scented oil, or use some bath salts in the tub and light some candles. Lie back, concentrating on the warm water calming you.

You could also make a little pouch filled with lavender and amethyst to carry with you if you are prone to getting angry. Or put a cluster of amethyst on your desk or in your living room.

Focus on the positive things in your life. Be creative about how you can meet challenges. Try not to get trapped in circular thinking. The past is past. It is done. There is nothing you can do about it, so let it go. Forgive the person, at least in your mind, even if you think they are wrong. Sending healing thoughts to others will help you overcome your own anger. Remember, the more you focus on negative energy, the less chance of success you will have at activating positive vibrations into your life.

Take a deep breath before each line of the affirmation and exhale slowly while speaking. Imagine all the anger running from every part of your body toward your fingertips. At the appropriate line, visualize your anger shooting from your fingertips, where you roll it into a ball. Throw the ball away.

For the second verse, close your eyes and imagine white light filling you with peace and contentment. Let your mind wander to decide how to tackle the problem at hand without losing your temper again. You should be able to think more clearly now.

> I call upon Spirit higher than me
> From this turmoil I face, please release me.
> Anger rages, boiling my blood
> Please send cooling guidance from your wisdom
>   above.
> Calm my nerves that quiver with fear,

Don't push away those that I hold dear.
Wrap me in comfort, keep frustration at bay
Roll my anger in a ball and throw it away.

Calm will center me
Deep breaths will focus me
From anger, release me
Peace will soothe me
I send light and love to that which frustrates me.
Harming no one, I give thanks, blessed be.

Concentration

Wearing a hematite ring can help ground racing thoughts and
aids in memory retention and concentration. You can make a
medicine pouch with Lily of the Valley, rosemary, spearmint,
and pieces of citrine, hematite, and quartz crystal.

Meditating sometimes helps us to concentrate. Pick a
tarot card or a stone or look at a picture and try to concentrate just on that one thing. Concentration is key to activating success in House Magic, so practicing a little bit each day
will help.

I call upon my Higher Self
To fill my life with love and good health.

Help me remember all that I should
Help me to concentrate, grounding is good.
Keep my thoughts from racing and flying free
This I ask and give thanks for,
Blessed be.

Courage

Carve the word *courage* into a red candle and let it burn.

Bloodstone, carnelian, and tiger eye are all great stones to activate courage. You can wear them, carry them in your purse, or put them on your desk. A medicine pouch might contain those stones and black cohash, columbine, and sweetpea.

I call upon the mighty Spirit
to fill me with logic and strength
To send my blood flowing vibrant and red
as I face the fear I truly dread.
Harming no one, I voice my thoughts
with clarity and grace.
Presenting a well-considered plan
I am able to save face.
Let understanding set me free.
This I ask and give thanks for, blessed be.

Dream Recall

There are many ways to activate dream recall. It can be as simple as asking your Higher Self to remember your dream upon your awakening.

Before you go to sleep, light a silver candle and ask your Higher Self to remember and help you understand your dream. Always keep paper and pen by your bed so that you can jot down notes immediately on waking up. Just words, or how you feel, or an image can help trigger the dream.

You can make medicine bags and dream pillows. In the bag you can include hops, horehound, kava-kava, rosemary, mugwort, lavender, citrine, lapis lazuli, and jade. You can place a gemstone under your pillow.

> I call upon power higher than me
> To bless my dream, bring a message to me.
> My dream will remain inside my head
> Long after I get out of bed.
> The meaning will be very clear
> I will act, I will persevere.
> Harming no one in my quest to receive
> This I ask and give thanks for, blessed be.

Harmony

We all dream of a home filled with peace and harmony. To help achieve this, put amethyst clusters around the house. Display balls of obsidian, fluorite, and amethyst to absorb chaotic energy. Light pink and blue candles.

Take a bath with rose or lavender oil or bath salts by the glow of pink candles. Meditate on white light filling your body with peace and harmony. Imagine yourself being calm and understanding. Think happy thoughts, of getting along with others, of really listening when people are speaking to you.

You could make a pouch with such items as amethyst, agate, rose quartz, tiger eye, gardenia, magnolia, rose, lavender, violet, and cumin.

> I call upon my Higher Self
> To fill my life with love and good health.
> Inner peace surges through my soul
> Each person I meet will feel more whole
> healing with peace and harmony.
> This I ask and give thanks for,
> Blessed be.

Health

When you have your health you can do anything. Sometimes life throws us a curveball and we are met with challenges of disease and disability.

To keep your health or improve on it, remember to drink eight glasses of water a day, walk as much as you can, do a bit of weight training and aerobics every week, eat a low-fat diet, and get plenty of rest. Common sense is the best remedy for health. If you are under the weather, call your doctor, midwife, or holistic health practitioner to rule out any serious consequences. Follow the treatment recommended for your ailments.

Any combination of amethyst, citrine, bloodstone, carnelian, aventurine, malachite, ash, camphor, coriander, St. John's Wort, and mistletoe are all good to include in a medicine pouch.

> Bless all those who touch this stone.
> Vibration remind us, we are not alone.
> Heal my heart, it aches with sorrow
> Heal my blood, my bones, my marrow.
> Flow blocked energy, surging high
> Let my dreams soar beyond the sky.
> Harm no one, bring love to all

All sacred energies please heed my call.
This I ask the powers that be
Thank you Motherfather, blessed be.

Love

You can use red or pink candles and burn them in your love corner on a Friday or during a new moon. The best stone to use for this affirmation is rose quartz.

> Beautiful stone I hold in my hand
> Surging with love at my command
> Higher Spirit I ask of you
> Please guide me in a way most pure and true.
> Harming no one as love comes to me
> This I ask and give thanks for.
> Blessed be.

New Baby

There is nothing like the joy of welcoming a new life into the world. Think about the pure innocence and possibilities this baby holds.

Bless stones such as rose quartz, apache tear, and quartz crystal and sew them into a little pillow filled with lavender or lilac to soothe, apple blossom for happiness, rose for love,

peace, and protection. You can sprinkle a bit of holy water on a baby while you say this prayer to protect them.

> Love and Light, I ask of you to fill this baby's heart
> with peace, joy, intelligence, and compassion:
> A whole and healthy start!
> Let this child grow wise with wonderment.
> Let this child embrace the Light.
> Let this child touch all those s/he meets with
> wondrous delight.
> Let this child harm no one, let no harm come this way.
> Thank you gentle spirit for blessing this child today.

New Home

You can hang your Chinese coins (see chapter 6) on the back of the front or main door. Use obsidian for protection, rose quartz for unconditional love, quartz crystal to absorb negative energy.

> This wondrous place I now call home
> Presents endless possibilities.
> With light and love please bless this place
> Let all my fears be swayed
> Let me weather hard times with wisdom
> Fill me with power to persevere.

Let all who cross this threshold
Leave with merriment and cheer
Harming no one in this quest
I ask and give thanks times three.

Prosperity

Light a green candle in your prosperity corner. The new moon is an excellent time to meditate on how you are going to create strategies to bring prosperity into your life.

Bless stones such as citrine and malachite and keep them in your prosperity corner. Keep citrine clusters on your desk and around the house.

You can put items such as citrine, malachite, quartz crystal, cedar, cinnamon, clove, ginger, honeysuckle, mint, nutmeg, or pine into a pouch.

I call upon my Higher Self
To fill my life with abundance and wealth.
The boundless energy of love and light
expands my life with eternal delight.
No harm shall come to anyone
This I pray, thy will be done.
Prosperity will come to me
This I ask and give thanks for.
Blessed be.

Rituals & Affirmations

Intent is key to all metaphysical work. If your intent is clear, you can have what you want.

You can fill your life with love and prosperity if your intent is honorable and you are focused. Focusing on goals can release blocks in other parts of our lives. Keep an open mind and open heart.

RITUALS

Visualize your goal. Speak your goal to the universe. Stay positive.

Remember that you can't affect another person's free will.

AFFIRMATIONS

Affirmations work best when you create your own.

THE DAYS OF THE WEEK

Perform your ritual on the day of the week that is associated with your goal to create the maximum energy to fulfill your intent.

SUGGESTED RITUALS AND AFFIRMATIONS

The examples provided here can be used as models for creating your own affirmations and rituals specifically focused on your intent. Be creative!

Collins Gem Zodiac Types. Glasgow: HarperCollins, 1993.

Crystal & Gem. London: Dorling Kindersley, 1991.

Cunningham, Scott. *Cunningham's Encyclopedia of Crystal, Gem & Metal Magic.* St. Paul, MN: Llewellyn Worldwide, 1988.

_____.*Cunningham's Encyclopedia of Magical Herbs.* St. Paul, MN: Llewellyn Worldwide, 1985.

Gerwick-Brodeur, Madeline, and Lisa Lenard,. *The Pocket Idiot's Guide to Horoscopes.* New York: Alpha Books, 1999.

Goldberg, Dr. Bruce. *Unleash Your Psychic Powers.* New York: Sterling Publishing Co., 1997.

Goldschneider, Gary, and Joost Elffers. *The Secret Language of Birthdays.* New York: Penguin Studio Books, 1994.

Hale, Gill. *The Practical Encyclopedia of Feng Shui.* London: Anness Publishing, 1999.

Kavasch, E. Barrie, and Karen Baar. *American Indian Healing Arts.* New York: Bantam Books, 1999.

Line, Julia. *The Numerology Workbook.* New York: Sterling Publishing Co., 1985.

Melody. *Love Is in the Earth: A Kaleidoscope of Crystals Update.* Wheat Ridge, CO: Earth-Love Publishing House, 1995.

Ravenwolf, Silver. *To Ride a Silver Broomstick.* St. Paul, MN: Llewellyn Worldwide, 1993.

_____. *To Stir a Magick Cauldron.*St. Paul, MN: Llewellyn Worldwide, 1995.

Reid, Lori. *East West Astrology.* Boston: Element Books, 1999.

Roob, Alexander. *The Hermetic Museum: Alchemy & Mysticism.* Koln: Taschen, 1997.

Skinner, Stephen. *Feng Shui.* Bath: Paragon, 1997.

Tognetti, Arlene, and Lisa Lenard. *The Complete Idiot's Guide to Tarot and Fortune Telling.* New York: Alpha Books, 1999.

Too, Lillian. *Essential Feng Shui.* New York: Ballantine Publishing Group, 1998.

_____. *The Fundamentals of Feng Shui.* Great Britain: Element Books, 1999.

Webster, Richard. *Chinese Numerology.* St.Paul, MN: Llewellyn Worldwide, 1998.

ACKNOWLEDGMENTS

I wish to thank all the people who assisted me with this manuscript, whether they were aware of their help or not.

First of all, thank you to everyone who shared their ideas and opinions with me. This includes clients, friends—especially Yvonne, Cecile, Nancy, Cathy, Sandra, Sara, and Julian, who listened to me and provided advice and support—family, and the authors of the books I used in my research. Thank you to the metaphysical teachers I've studied with over the years, including James P. Wells and Vivah.

I want to thank my business partner, Twilah, for all your information and support. To my agent, Lori, thank you for your hard work and your belief in me. To my children, thank you for putting up with my crazy hours and letting me get my work done. To my parents, thank you for all your love and support.

Thank you to Butch Miller for helping me with my manuscript and for helping me understand the foibles of human nature a tiny bit more.

Ariana

January 4, 2001

MOUNT VERNON CITY LIBRARY

Stephanie Beeley

Ariana is a writer, tarot counselor, and co-owner of the Two Stupid Witches company. She has been published in a wide variety of magazines and newspapers and has published several fiction novels under other names. She co-founded Two Stupid Witches with Twilah, another tarot counselor, in order to provide reasonably priced esoteric tools to clients. The name came about when they realized that individually, they are very intelligent women, but their combined energies sometimes make them lightheaded or spacy. The name reflects their sense of fun as they travel the fool's journey through life.

House Magic is chock-full of the sort of information that Ariana has shared with as well as learned from her clients. People are drawing from all disciplines to bring order to their lives, and Ariana has collected some of these ideas to share with her readers.

Ariana lives in Toronto with several creatures and a badly placed bathroom.

Conari Press publishes books on topics ranging from spirituality, personal growth, and relationships to women's issues, parenting, and social issues. Our mission is to publish quality books that will make a difference in people's lives—how we feel about ourselves and how we relate to one another. We value integrity, compassion, and receptivity, both in the books we publish and in the way we do business.

As a member of the community, we donate our damaged books to non-profit organizations, dedicate a portion of our proceeds from certain books to charitable causes, and continually look for new ways to use natural resources as wisely as possible.

Our readers are our most important resource, and we value your input, suggestions, and ideas about what you would like to see published. Please feel free to contact us, to request our latest book catalog, or to be added to our mailing list.

2550 Ninth Street, Suite 101
Berkeley, California 94710-2551
800-685-9595   510-649-7175
fax: 510-649-7190   e-mail: conari@conari.com
http://www.conari.com

MOUNT VERNON CITY LIBRARY